For information about permissions, licensing, or bulk orders, please contact:
Spector Creative, LLC
Greensboro, North Carolina
www.SpectorCreative.com

ISBN: 9798317095925
Printed in the United States of America
First Edition

1 2 3 4 5 6 7 8 9

Cover design, illustrations, and layout by Spector Creative
Hieroglyphic resources used in accordance with public domain and academic standards.

Library of Congress Control Number: *857320r52*

Dedicated to Brian King and Greg Miller who were the best companions trudging through the desert together. I'm still in de-nile on how great our Egypt adventure was!

Doodling with Purpose
Egyptian Hieroglyphs for the Modern Student

By
Scott D. Neitlich

Table of Contents

Introduction

Most books about Egyptian hieroglyphs are, let's face it, kind of... dry (was that a sand pun?). They tend to be academic tomes written for scholars, packed with footnotes, and written in a tone that feels more like a dissertation than a doorway to an ancient world. If you've ever picked one up, you might've felt more confused than inspired.

This book is different.

Doodling with Purpose is designed to bring the study of Egyptology to a modern audience—with pop culture references, clear diagrams, fun illustrations, and a tone that makes learning feel like an adventure, not a lecture. Whether you're a student, a casual history buff, or just someone who loves to draw, this guide is for you.

Why call it *Doodling with Purpose*? After working in corporate America for over 25 years, I found myself constantly waiting for meetings to start. Like many, I'd kill the time doodling cartoon characters in the margins of my notebook. One day, I thought—what if I could learn something while doodling? What if I could turn these idle moments into something meaningful?

That's when I discovered hieroglyphs. Not only are they fun to draw, but each doodle is a window into the beliefs, language, and daily life of one of the greatest civilizations in history. It was the perfect blend of art and intellect. My curiosity turned into a passion.

I was also deeply inspired by a life-changing trip to Egypt. Standing beneath the towering columns of Karnak, running my fingers across inscriptions in the Valley of the Kings, and floating down the Nile surrounded by temples covered in sacred symbols—something clicked. This wasn't just history, it was storytelling. It was visual poetry. And I wanted to bring that magic to others.

So here we are. This book will guide you—step by step—through the basics of reading and writing ancient Egyptian hieroglyphs. We'll start simple and gradually build toward full phrases and real inscriptions. You'll doodle, decode, laugh, and probably learn a few things you didn't expect.

Ready? Grab your pen. Let's doodle with purpose.

How to Use This Book

Welcome to *Doodling with Purpose*! This isn't your average textbook—it's a guided adventure through the ancient, beautiful, and wonderfully weird world of Egyptian hieroglyphs. Whether you're here for the history, the language, or just to draw some really cool owls, there's something in this book for you.

To help you get the most out of your journey, the book is divided into three parts:

Part 1: SECRET ORIGINS! The Story of Hieroglyphs

This section reads like an adventure. We'll travel from the banks of the Nile in antiquity through dusty tombs, into Renaissance curiosity cabinets, and finally to the libraries and breakthroughs of the 1800s. You'll meet the scholars, soldiers, and stone-chippers who cracked the code and brought hieroglyphs back to life. Think Indiana Jones meets *National Treasure*, but with more sand and fewer car chases.

Part 2: A LANGUAGE OF STONE: How to read Hieroglyphics

Now that you've got the backstory, it's time to dig into how this ancient script actually functions. We'll break down the alphabet, how words are formed, what determinatives do, and how to spot key glyphs. It's like learning the grammar of emoji—except the emoji are 3,000 years old and carved in stone.

Part 3: DOODLING 101: How to Draw Hieroglyphics

Here's where the fun really begins. In this section, you'll get hands-on with step-by-step guides for drawing many of the major glyphs. These are pulled straight from my personal hieroglyphic notebook (yes, it's a thing), and they're designed to be approachable, not intimidating. We'll cover over 100 of the most important uniliteral, biliteral, and triliteral signs—plus the ankh, the scarab beetle, and other rock stars of the hieroglyphic world.

Of course, you can read this book in any order you like. Some readers prefer to jump straight into the doodling with Part 3, while others love the historical context before picking up a pen. However you choose to tackle it, *this book is yours to explore*—flip, sketch, underline, reread. Just promise me you'll have fun. There is no right or wrong way to learn.

Enjoy the journey

PS: You will notice plenty of workbook lined pages throughout this book. You are encouraged to use these to doodle and glyph. You own this book, it is okay to draw in it!

Part 1: SECRET ORIGINS! The Story of Hieroglyphs

Chapter 1: From Glyphs to the ABCs

How Hieroglyphics Helped Shape the Alphabet You Use Every Day

Take a second and look at the letters on this page. The A's, B's, C's, D's. Familiar, right? Maybe even invisible because you've seen them so many times. But here's a wild thought: buried inside the history of those shapes is a winding, ancient path that starts not in Rome or Greece—but in Egypt.

Yes, the hieroglyphs you've been doodling throughout this book aren't just distant relics of a dead language. They're ancestral roots of the alphabet we use today.

This chapter traces that evolution—from Egyptian pictographs to the modern English alphabet—to show you how writing systems evolve, spread, and survive in surprising ways.

Writing as a Gift of the Gods

In ancient Egypt, writing wasn't seen as a human invention—it was a gift from the gods. The god Thoth was credited with creating hieroglyphs, which were known to the Egyptians as *medu netjer*, or "words of the gods." For thousands of years, hieroglyphs were used to record the wisdom of pharaohs, priests, engineers, and dreamers.

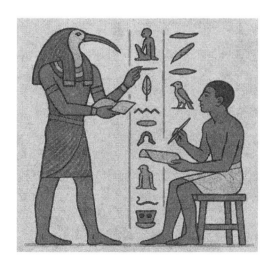

"I'll give you this pencil an paper, but the information is going to cost you."

But as time passed, empires rose and fell. And eventually, new groups—traders, settlers, conquerors—passed through Egypt and borrowed what they saw. And among the first to do that were the Phoenicians.

Phoenicians: The Alphabet Engineers

The Phoenicians were master traders and sailors based in what is now modern-day Lebanon. Around 1000 BCE, they developed a writing system that was revolutionary in its simplicity: an alphabet based on sounds. No pictures of gods, no sacred birds or eyes—just 22 characters, each standing for a single consonant.

But where did they get the idea?

Many scholars believe the Phoenician alphabet was directly influenced by Egyptian hieroglyphs, especially the simplified script called hieratic, which was used for daily record-keeping on papyrus. Some of the earliest known alphabetic writing (like the Proto-Sinaitic script) shows clear visual connections to Egyptian signs—just more abstract, simplified, and focused purely on phonetic sounds.

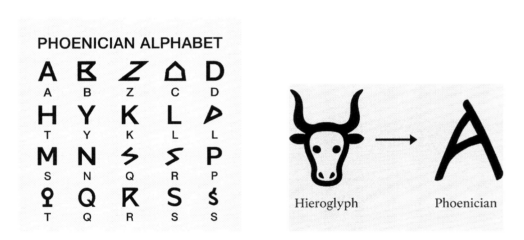

For example:

- The hieroglyph of an ox head (𓃾) likely evolved into aleph, the Phoenician letter for "A."

- The Egyptian house glyph (⌂) became beth—which gave us the letter "B."
- The camel glyph may have led to gimel, which became "G."

In other words, the Phoenician alphabet was hieroglyph DNA, reorganized for speed, trade, and practicality.

From Greece to Rome

The Greeks adopted the Phoenician alphabet around the 8th century BCE, making key changes along the way—most notably, the addition of vowels. Where Egyptian and Phoenician scripts focused mostly on consonants, the Greeks realized that marking vowel sounds made reading and writing more flexible and expressive.

They also reshaped the letters into the early forms we recognize today. Alpha, beta, gamma... you know where this is going.

From there, the alphabet traveled to Italy, where the Etruscans adopted it. And then, in the 7th century BCE, the Romans took hold of it and refined it into the Latin alphabet—the one we're using right now.

Your letter "A"? It started as an Egyptian ox. The letter "M"? It might trace back to mem, the Phoenician water sign—which itself may have been inspired by the Egyptian water ripple glyph (⎯). The letter "R"? It connects to resh, meaning "head"—just as the Egyptian mouth glyph (⌒) once symbolized sound and speech.

A Living Legacy in Your Notebook

So what does this mean for you, the modern scribbler, journaler, or glyph-doodler?

It means that every time you write in English, Spanish, French, or any language using the Roman (Phoenician) alphabet, you're writing with the descendants of hieroglyphs. That stylized letter on your keyboard has ancient DNA. The way you sign your name? That has echoes of scribes pressing reed pens into papyrus.

And when you write your name in hieroglyphs, you're not just copying ancient shapes—you're going back in time, participating in the lineage of writing that leads all the way to today.

The Loop is Closed

So here we are, full circle.

You are ready to start your journey by drawing little birds and eyes, learning that every symbol had sound and meaning. You will learn to write names, phrases, blessings. You will learn about sacred symbols, translated real inscriptions, and even explored how Egypt lives on in pop culture.

The writing system you use every day wouldn't exist the way it does without hieroglyphs. They're not some isolated system locked in a tomb. They are the roots beneath the tree of modern communication.

So the next time you text, type, or scribble in a notebook, remember: You are speaking with the voice of scribes. You are doodling with purpose. And you are carrying an ancient light into the modern world.

Chapter 2: The Mystery of the Glyphs

How the Ancient Language of Egypt Was Lost for Over a Thousand Years

The ancient Egyptians wrote everything. From tomb walls to shopping lists, tax records to sacred hymns, they recorded their lives in careful, pictorial detail. Names were preserved in royal cartouches.

Speeches were carved into temple pillars. Love poems, prayers, laws, and even jokes were all written down in the majestic script we now call hieroglyphics.
But then, something strange happened.

Despite being one of the most enduring writing systems in human history—used for over 3,000 years—Egyptian hieroglyphs suddenly disappeared. Not from monuments, of course. The glyphs remained carved into stone, perfectly legible and intact. But their meaning… was forgotten.

For more than 1,400 years, not a single person on Earth could read them.

The Silence of a Civilization

The fall of ancient Egyptian literacy didn't happen overnight. As Egypt became absorbed into the Greek-speaking world under the Ptolemies, and later into the Roman Empire, its own native writing system gradually faded into the background. By the 4th century CE, hieroglyphs had become associated almost exclusively with pagan temples and rituals. As Christianity spread through the region, those temples were closed, and with them, the last schools of scribal training vanished.

The final known hieroglyphic inscription was carved at the Temple of Philae in 394 CE. It was a short, reverent message to the gods—nothing out of the ordinary. But it would become the last time a hieroglyph was written by someone who actually understood what it meant.

After that, silence.

Generations passed. Egypt changed hands many times—Byzantine, Arab, Ottoman, and eventually European powers all left their mark. Tourists and conquerors alike stood in awe of the monuments, but no one could read the stories carved into them. The language of the pharaohs, the priests, and the people had gone dark.

Imagine discovering the Library of Alexandria but not knowing how to read. That's what Egypt had become: a monumental bookshelf of unreadable knowledge.

A Language Locked in Stone

People in the Middle Ages and early Renaissance didn't stop *looking* at hieroglyphs, but they misunderstood them completely. Lacking any key to decipher them, scholars invented interpretations based more on mysticism than linguistics. Many believed the glyphs were magical symbols—alchemical signs, astrological diagrams, or spiritual metaphors. They were treated like the runes of a lost civilization rather than components of a real language.

Some thought each hieroglyph stood for a full idea or moral principle. A lion symbolized strength. An eye represented God. A falcon meant divine protection. To a point, these associations weren't entirely wrong—but they were missing the crucial piece: the sounds. The phonetics. The grammar. The sentence structure.

They didn't understand that hieroglyphs could be *read*.

By the end of this book you will be able to read this! Cool huh?

Misguided Guesswork and Missed Clues

Even brilliant minds got it wrong. Renaissance thinkers such as Athanasius Kircher, a German Jesuit scholar, devoted years to studying the inscriptions. He compiled dictionaries of supposed meanings and wrote elaborate interpretations. But his work was mostly fantasy, layering Christian symbolism over ancient Egyptian concepts he didn't understand. He saw hieroglyphs not as letters, but as allegories.

The problem was that almost no one imagined hieroglyphs as a structured written language. They seemed too beautiful, too artistic, too symbolic to be phonetic. The idea that an owl could stand for "m," or that a seated man could represent the sound "z," didn't occur to most scholars of the time. Meanwhile, thousands of glyphs remained frozen in time—etched into temples, painted onto papyri, carved into the stone sarcophagi of long-dead kings. The words were right there. But the world had lost the instructions on how to read them.

A Puzzle Waiting to Be Solved

The truth is, the writing system itself had worked *too well*. Hieroglyphs weren't just sounds or letters. They were:

- Phonetic signs (like an alphabet)
- Symbols (like emojis)
- Determinatives (like hashtags to add meaning)
- Layout-based art (with direction and balance)

Without context, it was impossible to tell where one word ended and another began. Vowels weren't written. Word order changed based on artistic flow. And sacred traditions like honorific transposition meant names of gods or royalty were often placed out of grammatical order—making things even more confusing.

Trying to read hieroglyphs without guidance was like trying to play a video game with no tutorial, no manual, and the buttons scrambled on purpose.

The Echo of the Ancients

And yet... the monuments still stood. The Valley of the Kings. The temples at Karnak, Luxor, and Abu Simbel. The pyramid texts. The walls of tombs covered in prayer, poetry, and precise rows of silent symbols. They hadn't been destroyed—they'd simply waited.

People continued to sketch hieroglyphs in travel journals. Artists copied them onto canvases. Some wealthy collectors even brought obelisks and statues back to Europe. But the inscriptions on those artifacts were treated like decoration, not language. Without a cipher, they were no more readable than a lock without a key.

But the key was coming.

And it would arrive, fittingly, through an invasion.

Coming Up Next...

In Chapter 3 Napoleon arrives in Egypt—not just with soldiers, but with scholars, and he accidentally kicks off the rebirth of Egyptology. We'll meet the French thinkers who gave the glyphs their first modern name, "cartouches," because they looked like bullet casings—and we'll watch as the West starts to look at hieroglyphs not as mystery symbols, but as something that could be cracked.

Chapter 3: Napoleon in Egypt and the Return of the Glyphs

How a Military Invasion Sparked the Birth of Modern Egyptology

In 1798, the twenty-eight-year-old French general Napoleon Bonaparte launched a bold—and at the time, utterly baffling—military expedition into Egypt. Most people assumed it was a strategic move against Britain, a way to strike at colonial power by disrupting trade routes. But Napoleon had something else in mind too: a legacy.

He didn't just want to conquer Egypt. He wanted to study it.

Short Dead Dude.

What followed was one of the most unusual invasions in history. Alongside 40,000 soldiers, Napoleon brought with him a team of over 160 of France's brightest minds—scientists, artists, architects, engineers, linguists, botanists, and mathematicians. This group of civilian scholars became known as the Commission des Sciences et des Arts, and their mission was to document everything in Egypt— its people, plants, geography, animals, buildings, and especially, its monuments.

This wasn't just a military occupation. It was an Enlightenment-fueled intellectual invasion.

Discovering a Civilization in Stone

As Napoleon's army marched through the sands of Egypt, his savants began sketching and cataloging everything they saw. And what they saw stunned them: massive temples, crumbling obelisks, sphinxes, pylons, and walls upon walls of ancient writing. Hieroglyphs were everywhere—carved with precision, painted with color, and standing the test of millennia.

These weren't decorative flourishes. These were texts—statements from kings, records of offerings, prayers to gods, royal decrees. The French could sense it. They knew this script meant something. But, like everyone else in Europe at the time, they had no idea how to read any of it.

Still, they were captivated.

The team took thousands of measurements, created incredibly detailed illustrations, and produced accurate copies of inscriptions. Their work would eventually culminate in one of the most monumental publications of the 19th century: the *Description de l'Égypte*, a sprawling, multi-volume documentation of everything they saw. It was the first serious, modern academic engagement with the ruins of ancient Egypt.

But amidst all the temples and tombs, the scholars noticed something specific—something strange and consistent.

The Mystery of the Ovals

All across the walls of temples—especially those built during Egypt's later dynasties—the savants noticed small oval shapes, often standing vertically and filled with groups of hieroglyphs. These shapes didn't appear randomly. They occurred frequently, always containing tightly grouped symbols. Sometimes they were duplicated. Sometimes they appeared with a small horizontal line at the base.

The soldiers, who were less interested in sacred texts and more familiar with artillery, thought the ovals looked oddly familiar.

"They look like our gun cartridges," one of them remarked.

French gun cartridge circa 1790 and Egyptian Name cartouche.

In French, a cartridge (or bullet) is called a cartouche. And so, these mysterious name ovals—entirely unreadable but clearly important—were given their modern name: cartouches, thanks to a casual comment by a French soldier.

Ironically, these little shapes would prove to be one of the most important clues in cracking the entire system of hieroglyphic writing. They weren't just design elements—they were royal names. Markers of kingship. Identifiers of Pharaohs.

And now, the world had a name for them.

The Beginning of Egyptomania

When Napoleon's troops returned to France (well, those who made it back), they brought with them not treasure chests, but knowledge. The *Description de l'Égypte* stunned Europe. People were captivated by the detailed renderings of pyramids, temples, and—perhaps most of all—the exotic, mysterious hieroglyphs.

Though still unreadable, the glyphs began appearing everywhere: on furniture, architecture, jewelry, wallpaper, and paintings. European culture developed a full-blown obsession with ancient Egypt, a trend we now call Egyptomania. For the first time in centuries, people weren't just curious about the pyramids—they wanted to understand the civilization that built them.

But the mystery remained. How could a culture that recorded so much have left behind so little that was legible? How could a language, carved so deeply into the face of stone, have gone silent?

The answer was coming—but not from a scholar in a library. It would come from a stone slab, half-buried in a military outpost near the Nile.

Meanwhile, a Stone Waited

In the summer of 1799—just a year after Napoleon's invasion—French soldiers digging fortifications near the town of Rosetta (French for "little rose" from the local flowers) would uncover a strange, inscribed slab of black rock. It bore writing in three scripts. And one of them—Greek—was readable.

This is going to look great in the British Museum one day. Viva la French.

This find, which seemed like an afterthought at the time, would become the key to unlocking everything Napoleon's savants had seen. It would be the decoder ring that Egyptology had been waiting for.

And the cartouches—those mysterious bullet-shaped name tags—would become the first glyphs anyone truly read in over a thousand years.

Coming Up Next…

In Chapter 4 we'll explore the discovery of the Rosetta Stone, how it almost vanished into obscurity (again), and how it revealed a path forward to deciphering hieroglyphs.

Until then, remember: sometimes it takes a soldier's trench and a scholar's sketchbook to change the course of history. And sometimes, all it takes to name one of history's greatest puzzles… is a bullet.

Chapter 4: The Discovery of the Rosetta Stone

The Forgotten Rock That Taught the World to Read Again

In July of 1799, the summer sun beat down on a group of exhausted French soldiers digging defensive fortifications at Fort Julien, a crumbling structure near the Nile Delta town of Rosetta (modern-day Rashid). The French were still holding parts of Egypt under Napoleon's campaign, despite increasing British pressure. And these soldiers were doing what armies have always done when there's downtime: digging, reinforcing, building—anything to stay busy and ready.

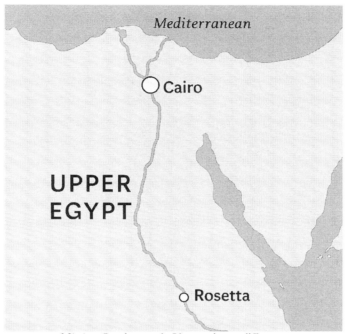

Missing: One large rock. If seen, please call Rosetta.

Then a shovel hit something hard. Not stone foundation. Not a wall. Something smooth. Heavy. And oddly marked.

What they uncovered was a flat, polished slab of dark granodiorite, about four feet tall and covered in ancient inscriptions. It was cracked across the top, likely from age or rough handling, but the rest was intact. One of the soldiers called over an officer. They had found something unusual—and it was covered in strange writing. No one present could read it, but one officer, Lieutenant Pierre-François Bouchard, recognized that the bottom third of the slab was written in Greek.

That meant this wasn't just another piece of broken architecture. This was something translatable. And it would become one of the most famous artifacts in human history: the Rosetta Stone.

Three Scripts, One Secret

Once scholars examined the slab more closely, they were amazed to find that the same text—presumably a royal decree—had been carved three times, each in a different script. At the top were elaborate, pictorial symbols unmistakably hieroglyphic. The middle section was a flowing, almost cursive script known as Demotic, the everyday writing system used in late-period Egypt. And the bottom, carved in the language of scholars and rulers, was ancient Greek.

One rock, three languages, one boring translation about taxes.

The genius of this layout was almost accidental. The decree had been written in three scripts to ensure that all of Egyptian society could read it. The priests would read the hieroglyphs. The administrators would read the Demotic. And the Hellenistic rulers and elite—descendants of Alexander the Great—would read the Greek.

But this one act of inclusivity, intended to communicate across Egyptian society in 196 BCE, would become the very reason the ancient Egyptian language could be resurrected centuries later.

From Obscure Find to Priceless Artifact

Bouchard immediately recognized the stone's potential value and sent it to Cairo to be examined by scholars attached to Napoleon's expedition. The French savants, already obsessed with cartouches and temple inscriptions, were astonished. A real, intact trilingual inscription—if the texts truly said the same thing—could offer them something they'd never had before: a side-by-side comparison between known language (Greek) and unknown language (hieroglyphs).

But the Rosetta Stone's journey was far from over. In 1801, when British forces defeated the French and negotiated their withdrawal, they included a clause in the Treaty of Alexandria demanding that all scientific and archaeological findings be handed over—including the stone.

There was, understandably, some drama. The French scholars didn't want to give it up. They considered it part of their intellectual mission, not a spoil of war. But ultimately, the British took possession, and the stone was shipped to London, where it was formally presented to King George III and deposited at the British Museum.

There it remains to this day—ironically, one of the most famous Egyptian artifacts never to reside in modern Egypt.

Deciphering the Undecipherable

Even with the Greek text at the bottom, the Rosetta Stone wasn't an instant translation tool. Scholars still didn't know how hieroglyphs worked. Were they letters? Words? Pictures? Magic symbols?
At first, many assumed hieroglyphs were purely symbolic—each one representing a concept or idea rather than a phonetic sound. This was how Renaissance thinkers had understood them for centuries. But now, with a matching Greek text, scholars could begin making direct comparisons. If they could identify proper nouns—like names of rulers—they could begin to piece together sound values.

One of the first to make progress was Thomas Young, an English scientist who correctly identified that the oval cartouches likely held royal names. He made headway into the Demotic script and realized it had a phonetic component—but it would be Jean-François Champollion, a brilliant French linguist, who would finally crack the code wide open.

The Rosetta Stone, it turned out, wasn't just a "stone with writing." It was a linguistic time machine. A frozen dictionary. A cipher. And like any good mystery, it had a starting point and a trail to follow— if only someone was clever enough to read the clues.

What the Stone Actually Said

By the time it was fully translated, the contents of the Rosetta Stone were—honestly—not that thrilling. It wasn't a prophecy, a spell, or the location of a hidden tomb. It was a fairly routine royal decree from the priesthood in Memphis, honoring Ptolemy V for his generosity toward temples and ordering those statues be erected in his name.

It included lines praising his rule, noting the tax reductions he had granted, and calling for annual celebrations in his honor. At the end, it specifically ordered that this decree be written in three scripts and placed in every major temple in Egypt.

And thank goodness for that last part—because this wasn't the only trilingual decree of its kind. But it was the one that survived.

What made it valuable wasn't what it said, but how it said it.

A Stone that Spoke for a Civilization

The Rosetta Stone bridged the gap between worlds. It connected the ancient and the modern, the sacred and the scholarly. And most importantly, it gave scholars something they had never had before: a way in.

In time, thanks to this humble-looking slab, the entire language of ancient Egypt would be slowly, painstakingly decoded. Every cartouche on every temple wall could now be revisited. Names, titles, prayers, and poems could be read once again—after more than a thousand years of silence.
It had taken a chance discovery in a military trench, a bit of luck, and the tireless work of countless scholars. But now, for the first time in over a millennium, the glyphs could speak.

Coming Up Next...

In Chapter 5, we'll meet Champollion, the young genius who cracked the code. Armed with curiosity, cartouches, and cleverness, he would do what no one else could: read the name of Cleopatra—and then open the floodgates to every other name, word, and phrase carved into Egypt's ancient stones. Ready to continue? Let's meet the man who finally listened closely enough to understand the whispers of the gods.

Chapter 5: Champollion Cracks the Code

The Moment the Glyphs Spoke Again

By the early 1800s, the Rosetta Stone had made its way to London, where it quickly became one of the most studied objects in Europe. Scholars and linguists crowded around it, sketched it, copied it, and sent plaster casts across the continent. It was clear to everyone that this stone had the potential to unlock the mysterious Egyptian language—but no one had yet found the key.

Then came Jean-François Champollion.

Born in 1790 in the town of Figeac, France, Champollion was a prodigy from the start. By age 11, he was already studying Latin, Greek, Arabic, Hebrew, and Syriac. By his teenage years, he'd added Coptic—the language of early Christian Egyptians—to his growing list. And that, it turns out, would be the secret weapon that set him apart from every other scholar trying to unlock hieroglyphics.

Champollion finds Hieroglyphics yet misplaces his hand.

Where others were trying to read the glyphs as abstract symbols, Champollion had a different suspicion: what if these glyphs actually recorded sound?
And what if the sounds they recorded had left a footprint—in Coptic?

Sounds Instead of Symbols

Most European scholars of the time were still under the impression that hieroglyphs were purely symbolic—like a secret code of pictures and ideas. The notion that the symbols might form a phonetic system—one based on sound—was radical. But Champollion, through his deep understanding of Coptic (which is descended from the ancient Egyptian language), began to notice connections. Some glyphs seemed to mirror the sounds of Coptic words. The more he compared, the more convinced he became: the ancient Egyptians weren't just carving pictures—they were writing a language.

And the Rosetta Stone wasn't just a political decree. It was a bilingual dictionary in disguise.

The Cartouche Strategy

Champollion focused his efforts on the cartouches—those oval rings of glyphs that Napoleon's soldiers had nicknamed after their gun cartridges. Based on earlier work by English scholar Thomas Young, Champollion zeroed in on the cartouches that he believed contained names. If he could decode a name, he could decode letters—and that would unlock phonetics.

One cartouche stood out: it appeared multiple times on temple inscriptions and had already been associated with the name Ptolemy, based on the Greek portion of the Rosetta Stone. By counting how many glyphs were inside the cartouche and comparing the name "Ptolemaios" in Greek, Champollion started making sound assignments:

- A square could be "P."
- A loaf shape might be "T."
- A lion might be "L."
- A double reed could be "I."
- An open mouth? Probably "O."

He began sketching out rough alphabet charts based on these guesses, which began to match names from other cartouches, including Cleopatra—a name found on temple walls in Dendera.

And then it happened.

The Breakthrough

On a September day in 1822, Champollion raced through his notes, scribbling new correlations. He had used cartouches from Cleopatra and Ptolemy to identify multiple repeated letters. He compared those to glyphs on other monuments and to Coptic words, slowly building a full working alphabet. In a surge of energy and certainty, he stood up, called to his brother, and shouted, "Je tiens l'affaire!" ("I've got it!")

Then, he collapsed. Quite literally. He fainted from the shock and excitement. The code had been broken—and the language of ancient Egypt was now, finally, readable.

It wasn't just about names anymore. Champollion could now identify words, grammar, structure. He understood that the script was a hybrid system—part phonetic, part symbolic, and always contextual. In short, he had cracked the hieroglyphic code.

That feeling you get when you beat Zelda for the first time.

A New Kind of Literacy

Champollion published his findings in a famous letter—*"Lettre à M. Dacier"*, presented to the French Academy of Inscriptions and Belles-Lettres on September 27, 1822. In it, he laid out his phonetic alphabet and described how he had used cartouches to decode not just names, but full words. He explained how some glyphs stood for sounds, others for ideas, and some served as determinatives to guide the reader toward the right meaning.

It was no longer a guessing game. It was now a language with rules, structure, and readable content. Tomb walls were no longer mute. Temple inscriptions could be read. Statues and sarcophagi could introduce themselves again after centuries of silence.

The Impact

Champollion's discovery turned Egyptology from a fringe fascination into a legitimate academic field. What had once been considered lost forever was now open for study. Over the next few decades, scholars used his method to translate thousands of texts—poems, letters, legal decrees, hymns, prayers, even personal notes scrawled by workers on temple walls.

Most astonishingly, Champollion had done all of this before the age of 32, and before the internet, before photography, before widespread travel. He had done it with plaster casts, sketches, dictionaries, and sheer brilliance.

He later traveled to Egypt to see the glyphs with his own eyes and confirm his theories in person, which only deepened his understanding. Sadly, his life was short. He died in 1832 at just 41 years old. But in that short time, he had resurrected an entire world.

Coming Up Next…

In Chapter 6, we'll take a look at how hieroglyphics have shown up in pop culture—especially in movies like *The Mummy* (1999), where ancient symbols light up screens and trigger traps. You might be surprised by what the glyphs actually say… and how often they're *real*.

Until then, remember: a single name can open a language. And sometimes, all it takes to hear the past is learning how to read it.

Oh, and for the record, here is how Cleopatra's name is decoded:

☑ **Hieroglyphs:**

(K L I P A D R A)

- ⌒ (*k*) – Basket with handle or hill (k)

- 🦁 (*l*) – Lion

- 𝄒 (*i/y*) – Reed

- ☐ (*p*) – Stool or whip (o)

- 𓅂 (*a*) – Vulture (glottal stop)

- ⌒ (*d*) – Hand

- ⌢ I – Mouth

- 𓅂 (*a*) – Vulture again

However because she is a "she", all females get a "t" added to the end of their name. It is silent, but it indicates the person is a female. It is noted here in parenesis.

K L E/A O P D R E/A (T)

Cleopatra's name in Glyphs. Note the silent T at the end.

Chapter 6: Hieroglyphs in Modern Times and Pop Culture

From Tomb Walls to Movie Screens—What the Glyphs Really Say

Once Champollion cracked the code, the doors to ancient Egypt didn't just open for academics. They opened for artists, writers, filmmakers, game designers, and dreamers. Almost overnight, Egypt's imagery—its gods, symbols, mummies, pyramids, and especially its glyphs—became irresistible creative fuel.

And so, over the past two centuries, Egyptian hieroglyphs have made their way into novels, cartoons, album covers, amusement park rides, fashion runways, and perhaps most dramatically… into movies.

But how accurate are those movie glyphs? And do they actually say anything? Or are they just mysterious squiggles thrown onto a wall to "look ancient"? As it turns out, the answer is… a little of both.

This chapter explores how ancient writing found its way into modern entertainment—and what those inscriptions actually mean when you take the time to translate them.

The Mummy (1999): Adventure, Action… and Real Glyphs?

Let's start with a fan favorite: *The Mummy* (1999), starring Brendan Fraser and Rachel Weisz. The film was a breakout hit—a campy, action-packed blend of Indiana Jones-style adventure and horror-tinged Egyptology. And yes, it features lots and lots of hieroglyphs.

Tomb walls are covered in them. Sarcophagi are encircled by glyph bands. Ancient spells are read aloud and translated on screen. You'd think most of this would be fantasy nonsense, right? Surprisingly, some of the hieroglyphs in *The Mummy* are actually real.

Prop designers consulted Egyptologists to ensure authenticity where possible. For example, in the chamber of Imhotep's resurrection, several inscriptions use actual Middle Egyptian text drawn from funerary spells and pyramid texts. One glyph band includes real references to the god Anubis, protector of the dead, and to phrases like "May your ka live forever" and "Given life, stability, and dominion."

Of course, the actors don't always pronounce things correctly. And not every glyph string is coherent. But as movie magic goes, *The Mummy* gets surprisingly close to the real deal.

Easter Egg Moment:

In one scene, Evelyn reads an inscription aloud: "Death is only the beginning." That phrase isn't directly lifted from an ancient source, but the glyphs surrounding it on the wall are based on actual Book of the Dead passages.

Hieroglyphs in Other Films and Games

The trend didn't stop with *The Mummy*. In *Stargate* (1994), glyphs are used to represent alien "gate coordinates," stylized to look like Egyptian symbols. While the language in the movie is fictionalized, the aesthetic is unmistakably based on real hieroglyphic structure—and the film helped reignite Egyptomania in the sci-fi crowd.

In *Assassin's Creed: Origins* (2017), Ubisoft took things to a whole new level. The game's "Discovery Tour" mode features real hieroglyphic inscriptions rendered in-game, and many can actually be translated using real linguistic principles. Glyphs appear on temple walls in full, and some even match real stelae that still exist today.

You can walk up to a pillar, examine a cartouche, and—thanks to the work of historians and language consultants—actually read what it says. That's not just cool—it's revolutionary educational design.

Do the Glyphs Say What the Movie Says?

Here's the thing: most audiences assume the glyphs in movies are either made up or purely decorative. And while that's true for some older or low-budget productions (we're looking at you, Saturday matinee mummy flicks from the '40s), many modern productions go out of their way to incorporate real text.

And once you've read this book—once you know your uniliterals, your cartouches, your offering formulas—you'll be able to start spotting actual words.

You'll notice when a king's name is written in a cartouche. You'll catch the glyph for "life" (☥), or "god" (𓊹), or "house" (□). You'll even start mentally translating words that whiz by onscreen. And yes—it's as satisfying as it sounds.

Try This at Home:

Rewatch *The Mummy* or *Moon Knight* and pause on any glyph-covered wall. Take a screenshot. Look for cartouches or groupings. Try matching them with your reference chart. You might be shocked how many real phrases are hiding in plain sight.

Beyond the Screen: Fashion, Music, and Memes

Hieroglyphs aren't just living in pyramids and Hollywood sets. They've made their way into pop culture on every level:
- Fashion designers have used glyphs in print designs, from dresses to sneakers. (Sometimes correctly. Sometimes… not.)
- Pop musicians like Katy Perry and Beyoncé have used Egyptian motifs, including glyphs, in music videos and stage performances—although not always with cultural sensitivity.

- Memes and TikToks now use glyph-style fonts to create mock "ancient scrolls" of online drama or personal wisdom. You'll even find hieroglyph filters that turn your name into stylized glyphs for profile pictures.

And while not every use is academically accurate, the important thing is this: people are still drawn to this writing system. It still inspires wonder. It still feels powerful.

So… Do They Actually Say Anything?

That depends. In your average T-shirt or novelty mug? Probably not.
In major Hollywood films, AAA video games, museum exhibits, and carefully crafted books like *Doodling with Purpose*? More often than you'd think.

And now that you know how to read them—even a little—you're in on the secret. You're one of the rare people who can look at an ancient wall, or a movie prop, or a comic book panel and say, "Hold on—I know what that says."

That's the magic of learning a lost language. It turns every museum visit into a treasure hunt. Every scene into a puzzle. Every symbol into a word, and every word into a voice.

Part 2: A LANGUAGE OF STONE: How to read Hieroglyphics

Chapter 7: Introduction to Ancient Egyptian Writing

Before emojis, before alphabets, before even paper itself, there was hieroglyphic writing.

The ancient Egyptians created one of the world's earliest and most enduring writing systems. Hieroglyphics—from the Greek meaning "sacred carvings"—was more than just a way to communicate; it was a way to connect with the gods, celebrate life, and prepare for the afterlife. Through these intricate pictures, Egyptians recorded prayers, laws, trades, jokes, poetry, and even shopping lists.

As we have mentioned in previous chapters, if you've ever watched *Moon Knight* or *The Mummy*, you've probably seen ancient walls packed with mysterious symbols. Hieroglyphs are everywhere in pop culture—from Indiana Jones dodging booby-traps in a hieroglyph-covered temple, to the inside of Wakandan tech from *Black Panther* mimicking ancient aesthetics with futuristic flair. Even if you didn't realize it, you've probably already had a brush with hieroglyphs.

In this chapter, we'll explore what hieroglyphs are, how they developed, and why they mattered so much to ancient Egyptian society. By the end, you'll understand that learning hieroglyphs isn't just about deciphering old texts; it's about discovering a visual language that is as meaningful as it is beautiful.

What Are Hieroglyphs?

Think of hieroglyphs as the OG emojis—small pictures packed with meaning. A single image can stand for a sound (like the letter "b"), an idea (like "sun" or "life"), or even an entire word. Sometimes they combine all three!

Not just a Journey cover band.

There are over 700 known hieroglyphic signs, though most everyday Egyptians didn't need to know them all. Many hieroglyphs are stylized images of real-world things: a vulture, a loaf of bread, a zigzag line for water. Unlike the alphabet you're used to, these aren't just letters. They're symbols with layers—like a meme with a double meaning. They could say what something *is*, *sounds like*, and *means*, all in one image.

Let's make this relatable. Imagine writing the word "fire" with a little flame icon 🔥. That's basically what ancient Egyptians did, except their flame might also be a syllable, part of a god's name, or a poetic metaphor. It's dense, it's expressive, and it's super visual. If you're a visual learner or love graphic novels, you're going to love this system.

The Three Types of Egyptian Script

You might think all ancient Egyptian writing looked like temple walls, but there were actually three major types:

1. Hieroglyphic: The iconic, detailed "art script" used in tombs, temples, and monuments. Think *National Treasure* or *Stargate* vibes.
2. Hieratic: A simplified cursive version, kind of like writing in longhand. It was used for scrolls, letters, and paperwork.
3. Demotic: An even more shorthand script used later in Egyptian history for everyday stuff. Kind of like texting in all abbreviations.

HIEROGLYPHIC   HIERATIC   DEMOTIC

| The iconic, detailed "art script" used in tombs, temples, and monuments. Think *National Treasure or Stargate* vibes. | A simplified cursive version, kind of like writing in longhand. It was used for scrolls, letters, and paperwork. | An even more shorthand script used later in Egyptian history for everyday stuff. Kind of like texting in all abbreviations. |

Basically, it's Egyptian block, cursive and short hand.

In this book, we're all about the hieroglyphic form. It's the most fun to draw, the most visually interesting, and the one you see all over popular culture. If you've seen the Rosetta Stone in the British Museum—or just online—that top row? That's hieroglyphics.

The Importance of Writing in Egyptian Society

To the Egyptians, writing wasn't just a convenience—it was sacred. They believed written words had power. That's not just metaphorical. They literally thought that writing someone's name gave it eternal life. This is why names are carefully written in cartouches (those oval shapes you see wrapped around text)—to protect and honor the person's spirit.

Writing played a central role in religion, politics, and even magic. Spells were written on tomb walls to help the deceased navigate the afterlife. Love letters were penned between nobles. Even curses were scratched into pottery shards. It was all about intentional communication—something we can still relate to today.

Scribes—the people trained to write—were like a cross between lawyers, artists, and tech support. They held respected jobs and were key to making the society function. Becoming a scribe was basically the ancient Egyptian equivalent of landing a job at Google or Pixar. It meant you were educated, trusted, and deeply plugged into the culture's beating heart.

Egyptians always drew the body facing forward because they believed if you did not draw it, that part of the body would not make it to the afterlife.

Hieroglyphs as Art and Language

Hieroglyphs weren't just for reading—they were meant to *look good*. Placement, symmetry, and visual flow were all carefully considered. Artists (often the scribes themselves) would arrange glyphs in squares and columns, flipping images so they faced each other, making sure the composition was beautiful. No sideways text dumps here.

This is where *doodling with purpose* comes in. Every glyph is its own little drawing, and as you learn them, you'll also learn how to arrange them into balanced, beautiful messages. It's like combining calligraphy with comic book layout. If you love bullet journaling, sketching fan art, or designing cool tattoos—this is totally your vibe.

In the next chapter, we'll start breaking down the building blocks: the uniliteral signs, a.k.a. the Egyptian "alphabet." They're the gateway to reading names, forming words, and decoding real ancient inscriptions. Spoiler: one of the first things you'll be able to do is write your own name in hieroglyphs. (Yes, like a theme park souvenir—but cooler.)

So sharpen your pencil or grab your stylus. Let's get hands-on with history.

Chapter 8: The Hieroglyphic Alphabet (Uniliterals)

The Original Emojis

If you've ever texted with a heart 🖤, fire 🔥, or laughing face 😂, congratulations—you already understand the power of symbolic communication. Ancient Egyptians did the same thing… about 5,000 years earlier.

Instead of a smiley face, they might draw an owl. Instead of a thumbs-up, maybe a loaf of bread. These weren't just pictures; they were part of a fully functional writing system. Welcome to the world of *uniliterals*, the one-sound wonders of ancient Egyptian hieroglyphs.

What Are Uniliterals?

Uniliterals are the closest thing ancient Egyptian has to an alphabet. There are 24 symbols, each representing a single consonant sound (like "b", "m", or "k"). They didn't write vowels (at least not the way we do), so these signs work more like the consonants in a game of Wheel of Fortune. You get the basic structure, and your brain fills in the blanks.

For example:

- 🦉 = m
- 🦅 = a or ' (a rough glottal stop)
- 🐛 = f
- 🦛 = Okay, no hippo… but there *is* a folded cloth that makes the sound s.

And for comparison to modern emojis above, here are the actual Egyptian symbols:

- 𓅓 = **m** (Owl)

- 𓅐 = ' **or a** (Vulture – glottal stop or "a")

- 𓆑 = **f** (Horned viper)

- 𓊃 = **s** (Folded bolt of cloth)

For the record, there is a "hippo" glyph, but it is not a sound glyph, it is a *determinative* which we will learn about in an upcoming chapter. For now just focus on the sound signs!

If you've seen *Stargate*, *The Mummy*, or even Marvel's *Moon Knight*, you've likely spotted hieroglyphs carved on temple walls or tomb entrances. What looks like art was also language—structured, poetic, and packed with meaning.

Pop Culture Connection:

Think of uniliterals like the letters you'd use to write a superhero's name in hieroglyphs. "Batman" becomes B-T-M-N. "Spider-Man" is S-P-D-R-M-N. (No vowels, remember?) Want extra flair? Draw them with little bats and webs in the margins. Boom. Hieroglyphic fan art.

Batman → B-T-M-N

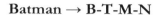

B   Foot

N   Water ripp

Batman in Glyphs:

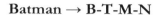

Spider-Man → S-P-D-R-M-N

S   Folded clo

D   Hand

N   Water ripp

r-Man in Glyphs:

Meet the Uniliteral Squad

Below is the classic roster of the 24 uniliteral signs. Each one has a sound value and a visual shape—sometimes based on animals, tools, or body parts.

Uniliteral Hieroglyph Chart

		Vulture	
╿		Reed leaf	Vowel-like glide sound
		Forearm	Glottal stop or voiced pharyngeal
⌋		Foot	Straightforward "b" sound
		Stool	Bilabial "p" sound
⌒	f	Horned viper	Sharp "f" sound
		Owl	Soft "m" sound, very common
ᔈᔈᔈ		Water ripple	Flowing "n" sound
		Basket with handle	Hard "k" or "c" sound
⌸	g	Jar Stand	Hard "g" (as in "go")
		Hand	Voiced "d" sound
		Cobra	"j" or "dj" as in "jam"
∏	s	Folded cloth	Soft "s" sound
	š	Pool or lake	"sh" as in "ship"
◠	t	Bread loaf	Feminine ending, unaspirated "t"

	Tethering rope		Emphatic "ch" or "tch"
	Placenta		Rough "kh" like in "Bach"
	Twisted flax		Strong breathy "h"
	Reed shelter		Light "h" sound
	Quail chick		"w" glide or semi-vowel
	Rounded loop		
	z Door bolt with crosspiec		Sometimes used for emphatic "z"

Each of these signs was both phonetic *and* visual—meaning the owl glyph stood for the "m" sound but also *meant* "owl" in context. It's a bit like how   can mean "snake" *and* be used as shorthand for "sneaky" or even "evil" in emoji-speak.

How They Work in Practice

Let's say you wanted to write the name *"Moses."*

In English, that's M-O-S-E-S. In ancient Egyptian, we drop the vowels and just keep the consonants. That leaves us with M-S-S.

So, you'd draw:

1. – **Owl**
    - o **Sound:** *m*
    - o **Meaning:** Represents the "m" sound; very common in names and vocabulary.
    - o **Visual:** Owl with detailed feathers and large eyes.

2. – **Folded Bolt of Cloth**
    - o **Sound:** *s*
    - o **Meaning:** Represents the "s" sound; foundational consonant.
    - o **Visual:** A folded piece of linen or cloth, stylized in a vertical curl.

3. Ꟁ – **Folded Bolt of Cloth (again)**
    o **Sound**: *s*
    o **Note**: Repeated for emphasis or phonetic completeness.

Boom. *Moses* in hieroglyphs.

(And yes, this is the same Moses whose name shows up in Egyptian records like *Thutmose*—"Born of Thoth," with "Mose" meaning "born of.")

🧠*Mind-Blowing Moment:*

Some scholars believe that names like *Ramses* and *Moses* share the same root. "Ra-mose" = "Born of Ra." The movie *Prince of Egypt* hits different when you realize the names weren't just labels—they were short-form poems.

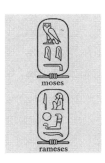

Egyptian texts.

Practice: Write Your Name in Hieroglyphs

Now it's your turn. Using the chart provided (in the appendix or exercise section), try writing your name in uniliterals. You'll probably have to drop vowels and just focus on the consonants.

Let's take a few examples:

- Emma → M-M
- Chris → K-R-S
- Jordan → J-R-D-N
- T'Challa → T-Ḥ-L (Close enough!)

Don't worry about accuracy right now—it's more important to get comfortable *thinking like an Egyptian*. Visual, phonetic, and stripped down to essentials.

🎨*Creative Challenge:*

Design a "name badge" in hieroglyphs for your favorite character—Black Panther, Lara Croft, Indiana Jones. Use your own style and doodles to bring it to life.

Why It Matters

Learning the uniliterals is like picking up the basic keys to the language. Once you've got these down, you can start building words, recognizing names, and decoding real inscriptions.

Just like learning the alphabet as a kid unlocked the world of reading, mastering these 24 glyphs opens up a doorway into ancient temples, tomb walls, and museum exhibits around the world.

And honestly? It makes you look *really cool* next time you're at a museum or watching *Stargate* reruns with your friends.

Coming Up Next…

In Chapter 8, we'll level up to biliterals and triliterals—the power combos of Egyptian writing. Think of them as hieroglyphic "cheat codes" that let you say more with fewer symbols. It's like moving from single notes to full chords.

Single	**Sound**	**Glyphs**					
(glyph)	ꜣ	(glyph)	i̓	(glyph)	ꜥ		
(glyph)	B	(glyph)	k	(glyph)	ḫ		
(glyph)	ḥ	(glyph)	f	(glyph)	N		
(glyph)	R	(glyph)	p	(glyph)	S		
(glyph)	Š	(glyph)	g	(glyph)	Q		
(glyph)	T	(glyph)	ṯ	(glyph)	D		
(glyph)	ḏ	(glyph)	w	(glyph)	ḥ		
(glyph)	Z	(glyph)	y				

Start here! Your best way to begin learning Egyptian is to learn these glyphs above.

Chapter 9: Bilaterals and Trilaterals

When Letters Team Up to Say More

If uniliterals are the alphabet of hieroglyphics, biliterals and triliterals are like syllables—or even cheat codes. Instead of representing just one sound, these glyphs combine two or three consonant sounds into a single symbol.

Think of it like this:

- "B" = uniliteral
- "BL" = biliteral
- "BLK" = triliteral

The ancient Egyptians were writing efficiency masters. Instead of stacking multiple signs to spell out every sound, they often used one glyph that packed multiple consonants. It's like going from spelling out "laugh out loud" to just typing LOL—faster, cleaner, and still totally readable (if you're in the know).

Why Use Biliterals and Triliterals?

You might be wondering: if they already had a full set of uniliterals, why use these combos?

Simple: space and style. Hieroglyphs were often written in tight spaces (like tomb walls or jewelry) or arranged to be aesthetically pleasing. By using fewer glyphs to say more, scribes could save space, balance the composition, and still convey full meaning.

Pop Culture Reference:

Think about Batman's logo. One image = a whole identity. Egyptian scribes did the same. A single glyph could convey a whole sound cluster, like "nfr" (meaning *beautiful* or *perfect*), which is famously shaped like a heart and windpipe. Now *that's* graphic storytelling.

pr

ḥtp   k³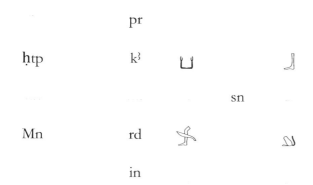

                              sn

Mn   rd

                              in

These are actual symbols you'll encounter often, especially in names like:

- Tutankhamun → Includes "ankh" (life) and "amun" (the god Amun)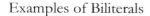

- Ramses → "Ra-mes-su" = Born of Ra

Quick Decode:
The name *Ramses* contains the triliteral ms ("born of") and Ra (the sun god). It's like a mini myth encoded into a name—basically an origin story like "Son of Krypton" or "Daughter of Themyscira."

Examples of Triliterals

Nfr   ḥtp

Nswt   ḏd³

k³ʿ   b³k

Notes:

- All these signs have **triliteral phonetic values**.
- Many are symbolically rich:
    - **nfr** = beautiful/good/perfect
    - **ḥtp** = offering/peace
    - **ḫpr** = to become (the scarab beetle!)
    - **ʿnḫ** = life
    - **wʾs** = power/dominion

Triliterals are glyphs that pack three consonants into one symbol. These are a bit rarer but super important for decoding deeper meanings.

Again, these symbols appear all over monuments, tombs, and even amulets worn for protection and power.

Doodling Tip:

Because biliterals and triliterals are complex images, they're extra fun to draw. They often combine recognizable body parts, tools, or objects. Try drawing them stylized in your own way—kind of like designing your own Pokémon based on Egyptian themes.

How to Use Them in Writing

Here's the cool part: when scribes used biliterals and triliterals, they often still added uniliteral signs afterward to reinforce pronunciation. These are called phonetic complements.

Let's take nfr as an example:

1. The triliteral glyph for "nfr" (heart + windpipe) is used.
2. Then they might add the uniliteral for "r" afterward—just to be extra clear.

It's like ancient spell-check.

Modern Analogy:

Imagine writing the word "Knight," but then drawing a little sword just to reinforce the theme. Redundant? Maybe. Cool? Definitely.

Practice Time

Try writing these words using biliterals and triliterals:

1. Per-Ra (House of Ra) – pr + Ra glyph
2. Nefertiti – nfr + t + t + (you'll get the hang of it)
3. Ankh-Mesut (Born of life) – ꜥnḫ + msw.t

Don't worry if this feels like a puzzle at first. It is! But one that's worth solving.

Creative Challenge

Design your own superhero name or title using a mix of uniliterals and biliterals. For example:

- "Shadow Blade" → sh-d + b-l-d
- "The Flame Keeper" → ḫ-t + ḥb

Draw the glyphs, make a logo, and write out a translation key. This is how modern storytelling meets ancient code!

Coming Up Next...

Now that you're armed with uniliterals, biliterals, and triliterals, you're ready to read *real* hieroglyphic words. In Chapter 10, we'll dive into determinatives and ideograms—the signs that add clarity, category, and context to everything you've learned so far.

Until then, keep decoding… and keep doodling with purpose.

Chapter 10: Determinatives and Ideograms

When Pictures Say More Than Words

If you've ever seen a comic book panel where a character has a little   above their head to show an idea—or a   emoji next to something to suggest danger—you already understand what determinatives do.

In Egyptian hieroglyphics, determinatives and ideograms are like the secret sauce. They're what turn a string of consonants into something clear and specific. Without them, you'd be guessing whether "bat" means a flying mammal, a baseball tool, or a spooky vampire reference. (And yes, the Egyptians had to deal with similar ambiguity—even without Dracula.)

What Is a Determinative?

A determinative is a non-phonetic glyph added at the end of a word. It doesn't represent a sound. Instead, it tells you *what kind* of word you're looking at—like a visual hashtag.

Let's say you're reading the word *nfr* (which, as you remember from Chapter 3, means "beautiful"). The scribe might add a seated man determinative to tell you it's referring to a person, or maybe a temple icon to signal a place.

It's like adding context clues in emoji form:

- = Travel
- = Food
- = Person

Movie Moment:

Think about subtitles in *The Mummy* when ancient spells are being read aloud. Without the determinatives, the meanings would be vague or misleading. They're the ancient version of "this is what we mean," and scribes used them *a lot*.

Common Categories of Determinatives

Here's a quick look at some of the most common determinative signs:

Meaning	Meaning	Meaning
City/Town	Foreign land	Sky/Heaven
Tree/Wood	Cloth/Linen	Gold/Precious

The Egyptians didn't have punctuation, boldface, or italics. So determinatives were their way of saying, "Here's what we mean—no guesswork needed."

What's the Difference Between Determinatives and Ideograms?

Good question!

- A determinative adds context but doesn't make a sound.
- An ideogram is a picture that stands for the whole word *and* its meaning.

For example:

- The word for *sun* is "Ra"   —and the sun glyph can be both the sound "ra" and the full concept of the sun god himself. It's kind of like the Superman "S" standing for both his name and what he represents.

Geek Alert:

Ideograms are like logos in pop culture. Think of the *Avengers* "A" or Batman's bat symbol. One image, multiple layers of meaning. That's what an ideogram does in ancient Egyptian.

Why It Matters for Reading and Writing

You can think of determinatives and ideograms as visual grammar. They:

1. Help clarify words that sound alike (homophones).
2. Make texts easier to scan and understand.
3. Bring an added layer of symbolism and cultural nuance.

Without them, reading hieroglyphs would be like texting with only consonants and no context:

- "BRN" = Born? Burn? Baron?
- "SNK" = Snack? Snake? Sneak?

The determinative clears all that up by saying, "Oh, it's the one with the snake icon—so it's *snake*."

Practice Exercise: What Does It Mean?

Let's say you see this sequence of glyphs:

+   +   +

You know from earlier chapters that:

- = M
- = S
- = Person determinative

So that's M-S-S + person = someone's name, probably "Mose" or "Moses."

Now imagine it ends with   instead: that shifts the meaning toward a place—perhaps a temple or city called "MSS."

The determinative changes the *entire interpretation*. It's like the difference between *Wakanda* (a place) and *Wakandan* (a person from that place).

Creative Challenge

Try writing this short sentence in hieroglyphs:

"A beautiful woman speaks to a god."

You'll need:

- "nfr" (beautiful) + woman determinative
- "rḏw" (to speak) + action determinative
- "nṯr" (god) + god glyph

$\frac{†}{☦}$ = *nfr* ("beautiful")

𓁐 = Seated woman determinative (used for feminine words)

Draw each word with the proper determinative and see how much more clear and epic it becomes.

Bonus Style Tip: Make your arrangement look like a comic strip panel—remember, Egyptian writing is also a visual art form!

The second type of non sound sign we need to review is an *ideogram*.

So What's an Ideogram with you, Anyway?

Okay, now that we've covered determinatives—those handy little context-clues that tag along at the end of a word like the "emoji" of the ancient world—it's time to meet their slightly flashier cousin: the **ideogram**.

If determinatives are like the punctuation mark at the end of a sentence, **ideograms** are the full-on headline.

Ideograms = What You See *Is* What You Get

An **ideogram** is a glyph that *is* the word it represents. Literally. Like, if you wanted to write the word

"owl," you'd just draw the owl glyph: 𓅓 — boom! That's both the *picture* and the *word*. No extra letters required. It's the ancient Egyptian version of pointing at an emoji and going, "Yeah, that's exactly what I mean."

So while phonetic glyphs (uniliterals, biliterals, triliterals) **sound out** the word, i
word.

Think of it like this:

- Phoı ; out "C-A-T"
- Ideo 𓃠 ← and that's your word

Determinatives vs. Ideograms — Let's Break It Down

Position	Usually at the end of a word	Can be the whole word by itself

Why Ideograms Are Awesome

They're visual shortcuts. They let you skip the spelling and get right to the point. Want to say "sun"? Just draw the sun disc: ⊙. Want to write "king"? Use the glyph of a seated man with a crown: 𓀭.

Ancient scribes didn't just love these because they were efficient—they loved them because they *looked cool.* Hieroglyphs were meant to be art, not just text. And ideograms are the bold graphic design elements in this ancient visual language.

How to Use Them Like a Pro

When you see a glyph all by itself and it *makes sense visually*, there's a good chance it's being used as an ideogram. Some glyphs can **double** as both phonetic signs *and* ideograms depending on context, which is where practice and familiarity come in.

Examples:

- 𓂋 can mean the sound "r" (like in "Ra") *or* it can be used as the ideogram for "mouth."
- 𓆣 is both the beetle for "kheper" (to become) and the *word* for transformation.

don't worry if it seems confusing at first. Think of it like comic books: the same visual might be part of the word balloon one time and part of the artwork the next. You'll get the hang of it.

Pro Tip: Spotting Ideograms in the Wild

If a glyph is used *alone*, or it's repeated for emphasis, chances are it's acting as an ideogram. Watch for things like:

- ⟃ (hand) meaning "give"

- ⌒ (loaf) meaning "bread" or the feminine marker

- ⊙ (sun disc) meaning "day," "sun," or "Ra" depending on context

You'll also see them in **royal cartouches**, **temple inscriptions**, and pretty much every tomb wall in Egypt.

Final Thought: Glyphs Are Multi-Taskers

Just like how Chris Evans can be both the Human Torch *and* Captain America, many hieroglyphs pull double (or triple!) duty. One moment they're a letter, the next they're a word, and sometimes they're just there for flair.

Ideograms are what make Egyptian writing both a language and an artform. And the more you learn to spot them, the more you'll realize—these ancient doodles really *did* have purpos

Coming Up Next…

Now that we've unlocked the mystery of determinatives and ideograms, you're ready to tackle full hieroglyphic sentences. In Chapter 11, we'll break down hieroglyphic grammar—the sentence structures, gender rules, and how Egyptians said "I love you" or "Pharaoh wins again."

Spoiler: They didn't always do it in the same order we do.

Until then, keep decoding, keep doodling, and keep speaking ancient truths—visually.

Determinatives

People   Women

Actions   Creatures   Abstract
or violence   ideas

People   Civil   Logos

Determinatives help you determine what the word is. Sure helps when there are no vowels!

Chapter 11: Hieroglyphic Grammar Basics

How to Speak Like a Pharaoh (In Pictures)

Okay, so now you can recognize the Egyptian "alphabet" (uniliterals), their shortcuts (biliterals and triliterals), and the visual clues (determinatives and ideograms). That's a solid toolbox. But how do you actually say something in ancient Egyptian?

Time to put it all together.

Think of grammar as the stage direction of language. It tells us who's doing what, to whom, and how. Without grammar, even the best glyphs get lost in translation.

Pop Culture Example:

Ever try watching *Star Wars* in Yoda-speak? "Strong with the Force, you are." It's quirky but understandable. Egyptian sentence structure is kind of like that—unfamiliar at first, but totally learnable once you know the rhythm.

Word Order: Verb Comes First!

In English, we usually go:
Subject – Verb – Object

"Leia (subject) loves (verb) Han (object)." (I know…)

But in Egyptian hieroglyphs, it's often:
Verb – Subject – Object

"Loves Leia Han." (know I…)

Yep, Yoda would be proud.

Grammar Hack:

The verb kicks off the sentence like the opening scene of a movie—*action first*. So any time you see a verb glyph leading the line, you know something's going down.

Gender and Number: Ancient Grammar Rules

Just like in Spanish or French, Egyptian nouns have gender (masculine or feminine) and number (singular or plural).

Gender:

- Masculine words often end with nothing.
- Feminine words often end in -t (marked by a loaf of bread g).

Example:

nfr –

- **Meaning:** *Beautiful, good, perfect* (masculine)
- **Glyph Description:** Heart and windpipe
- **Pronunciation:** *nfr*

nfrt –

- **Meaning:** *Beautiful* (feminine form)
- **Additional Glyph:** Loaf of bread (.) = "t" sound, often marks feminine nouns

Number:

- Plural is usually marked with three strokes | | | (like tally marks).
- Dual (for things that come in pairs, like eyes   or arms   ) has its own special suffix, often ending in "-wy."

    Word Time: "eye" = *irt*
"eyes" = *irtyw* + | | |

That's right—hieroglyphs could even count for you.

Pronouns: Who's Talking?

Egyptians had personal pronouns, but they didn't always write them like we do. Instead, they might use a name, a title, or even just a determinative. Here are some basic ones:

You (m.)		line "you" – "n" + "t" + "k"
He / him		d viper; used as suffix in verbs
We / us		ater ripples – dual/plural "we"

Notes:

- These **pronouns often appear as suffixes** in verb constructions, rather than as stand-alone words like in English.
- The **"ink"** form ( ) is one of the few pronouns used in **independent subject** position, similar to "I am."

Hero Example:

"I am Batman."
In Egyptian it might be: *ink Bat-man* (with a glyph for "man" and a bat if you want to doodle for fun).

Verb Forms: Action, Egyptian Style

Verbs were the engine of every sentence, and the Egyptians had multiple tenses—though they didn't think of them as past, present, future like we do. Instead, they cared about *completed* vs *ongoing* actions, and whether something was declarative, negated, or emphatic.

Let's keep it simple:

Verb Form Breakdown (with Hieroglyphs)

For a full list of common verbs see Appendix I.

1. **sḏm.f – "He hears"**
   o **Glyphs:** 𓂋𓏤𓅓𓄿 𓆑
   o **Explanation:** Present or simple/perfective aspect.
   o **Structure:** Verb stem + subject suffix (*he* = 𓆑).

2. **sḏm.n.f – "He heard"**
   o **Glyphs:** 𓂋𓏤𓅓𓄿 𓈖 𓆑
   o **Explanation:** Past tense construction.
   o **Structure:** Verb + past marker (𓈖) + suffix pronoun. Think of the past marker water glyph as "ed" in English. Walk becomes walked and so on.

3. **sḏm.tw.f – "He is heard"**
   o **Glyphs:** 𓂋𓏤𓅓𓄿 𓏏𓅱 𓆑
   o **Explanation:** Passive voice.
   o **Structure:** Verb + passive particle (tw) + subject

Think of verbs like movie shots:

Hieroglyphic Verb Forms as Film Scenes

sḏm.n.f	𓅓𓄿 𓈖 𓆑	"He heard" (past)	*Flashback*

A Simple Sentence: Let's Build One!

"The king gives bread."

Glyph Order (Verb-Subject-Object):

- ⌐𓏤 (*di*) – "gives" – hand glyph

- 𓏎𓇓𓂋 (*nswt*) – "king" – seated man with crown

- 𓏐 (*t*) – "bread" – loaf symbol

Full sentence in Egyptian order:

⌐𓏤 𓏎𓇓𓂋 𓏐

→ *di nswt t*

If you wanted to add flair, you'd use determinatives for person and food, and maybe throw in honorifics or divine names.

Speech Bubble Style:

Draw a comic-style panel of a Pharaoh handing out bread. Caption it with hieroglyphs. Boom— ancient grammar meets graphic novel.

Practice: Make a Meme

Here's your creative challenge:

Write the sentence "The cat sees the snake."
You'll need:

- Verb: *see* = m^3
- Subject: cat = *miw*
- Object: snake = *djd*

Arrange them:
m^3 miw djd

"The cat sees the snake."

Egyptian word order: Verb – Subject – Object

- 𓅓𓄿 (*m³*) – "sees"

- ⸗ℓℇ (*miw*) – "cat"

- ⸗⸗ (*djd*) – "snake" (curled cobra, repeated to represent full biliteral spelling)

Full sentence in hieroglyphs:

⸗⸗ ℓℇ ⸗⸗

→ *mꜣ miw djd*

Add determinatives (animal for cat, snake glyph), and maybe draw it like a "Tom & Jerry" skit in ancient glyph-style panels.

Coming Up Next…

In Chapter 12, we'll talk about layout, direction, and artistic balance—because Egyptians weren't just great writers; they were *designers*. We'll learn how they arranged glyphs to be read correctly and look amazing, whether on a tomb wall or a tourist T-shirt.

Until then, keep sketching, keep practicing, and remember: grammar isn't a buzzkill—it's what lets you write like a Pharaoh.

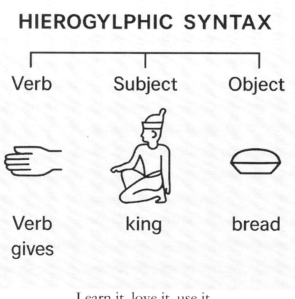

HIEROGYLPHIC SYNTAX

Verb	Subject	Object
Verb gives	king	bread

Learn it, love it, use it.

Chapter 12: Direction and Layout of Hieroglyphs

How to Read a Wall Like a Designer

Let's be honest—when you first look at a wall of Egyptian hieroglyphs, it feels like decoding *The Matrix*. The symbols seem to go in all directions, and it's hard to tell where to start or what's upside down.

The good news? There's a method to the visual madness. Egyptian writing wasn't just language—it was layout art. Think of it like the panel flow in a comic book or the symmetrical balance of a movie poster. It had rules, rhythm, and visual poetry baked in.

Pop Culture Example:

Imagine watching *Avengers: Endgame* with the scenes out of order. Confusing, right? The Egyptians knew that visual flow mattered. Their texts weren't just read—they were *experienced*.

Which Way Is This Thing Going?

Unlike English, which is strictly left-to-right, hieroglyphs could go:
- Left to right
- Right to left
- Top to bottom

The direction is determined by which way the glyphs face.

Reading Rule:

Faces point toward the beginning of the line.
So if birds, humans, and animals are all looking left—start reading from the left.
Glyphs were rarely flipped just for fun. It was always intentional—often done to maintain artistic balance or fill awkward spaces in a layout.

So basically you can go up and down, left to right, but not back in time.

Why Did They Change Direction?

Think of hieroglyphs like tiles in a mosaic or Tetris blocks. Ancient scribes wanted them to:
1. Fit the space.
2. Look balanced and beautiful.
3. Flow harmoniously.

This wasn't just for aesthetics—it was sacred. The writing was meant to honor the gods, the dead, or the pharaoh. So it had to look *just right*.

Design Vibes:

It's kind of like making a perfectly symmetrical Instagram carousel or designing a tattoo sleeve where each piece flows into the next. Ancient Egyptians were basically OG layout artists.

Grouping Glyphs: The Art of Block Stacking

Hieroglyphs weren't written in a straight line like typed text. They were grouped into neat blocks, often forming squares or rectangles.

Here's how they grouped them:
- A tall glyph (like a reed) could sit beside a short glyph (like a loaf).
- A bird could perch above a ripple of water.
- A set of three short glyphs might stack to form a column.

The goal? Keep everything tight, clean, and symmetrical. Think of it like fitting images on a comic book cover so the title and characters all fit perfectly.

When reading glyphs arranged in a box, you will always read left to right (or right to left depending on the way glyphs face) and THEN up to down. Here is an example of the correct order when dealing with a block of glyphs:

Into the eyes, top to bottom. And you thought English was weird.

Doodle Tip:

When you're writing glyphs, imagine placing them into invisible grid squares. Stack small ones and pair tall ones—just like a game of visual Tetris.

Honorific Transposition: Put the Gods First

Here's something really cool—and very Egyptian. Even if a name or subject *should* come later in a sentence, scribes would often move gods or royalty to the front out of respect. This is called honorific transposition.

For example:

"Ra loves the king"

Grammatically: "Loves Ra the king" → di Ra nswt

But they might write it visually: Ra di nswt

They flipped the layout to honor the god, even if the grammar was rearranged. That's like starting a movie with the cameo of the main villain just to show how powerful they are.

Sample Layouts
        you might see:
     ₋ayout (Left to Right or Right to Left)

← Read this way if the faces point left.
Vertical Layout (Top to Bottom)

↓ Read this way if glyphs are stacked.
These layouts appear on tomb entrances, stelae (commemorative slabs), and even amulets. They weren't just messages—they were sacred visuals.

Real World Example:

The inscriptions on the walls of Tutankhamun's tomb flow in vertical columns, each beautifully balanced, each read top to bottom, with symbols grouped for elegance.

Practice Challenge: Build a Balanced Block
Try writing this phrase: "Life to the king."

- Life = *ankh* (☥)
- To = *n* (water ripple)
- King = *nswt* (crowned figure with crook and flail)

Stack them neatly in a vertical block, balancing large and small glyphs.

Add a determinative if you like—and don't forget to face them in the right direction!

Bonus Creativity Tip: Try redrawing the phrase like a phone wallpaper design, keeping the symmetry and sacred feel.

Coming Up Next…

Now that you know how to *write like an Egyptian designer*, you're ready to tackle real-world inscriptions. In Chapter 13, we'll look at names, titles, and cartouches—those fancy ovals that seal someone's name with royal status (and maybe eternal life).

Soon, you'll be reading and writing names like Cleopatra, Thutmose, and maybe even your own—with a hieroglyphic crown on top.

Until then, keep balancing your blocks, and keep doodling with purpose!

Chapter 13: Names, Titles, and Cartouches

Sealing Your Name in History

You've probably seen them—oval-shaped loops of hieroglyphs surrounding the name of a pharaoh or a royal. They're called cartouches, and they're basically the ancient Egyptian equivalent of putting a name in lights. But instead of Broadway marquees, these ovals promised something even cooler: eternity.

Real-World Moment:

On the walls of the Karnak Temple and tombs in the Valley of the Kings, you'll find cartouches for Tutankhamun, Ramses, and Seti. Their names are *still* being read thousands of years later. That's legacy.

Tutankhamun (⬭⬭🦅⬭⬭🦅☉)

- **Transliteration:** *Twt-ʿnḫ-ỉmn*
- **Meaning:** "Living image of Amun"

- **Glyph Features:** Loaf (⬭), Ankh (☥), Reed (𓇋), and Sun disk (☉)

Ramses (⬭⬭𓄿🦅⬭)

- **Transliteration:** *Rʿ-ms-sw*
- **Meaning:** "Born of Ra"

- **Glyph Features:** Sun disk (☉), Child (𓄿), Sedge/reed (⬭)

Seti (𓊃⬭𓇋)

- **Transliteration:** *Sty*
- **Meaning:** "Of Set" (the god Seth)

- **Glyph Features:** Folded cloth (𓊃), Bread (⬭), and Reed leaf (𓇋)

What Is a Cartouche?

As noted in part 1 part this book, a cartouche is an elongated oval with a line at the bottom, wrapped around the hieroglyphs of a royal or divine name. It signaled that this person was important, usually royalty. It also offered magical protection—writing your name in a cartouche was believed to secure your identity for the afterlife.

Think of it as:

- A crown for your name
- A royal nametag
- A username that unlocks immortality

We don't need no stinkin badges. We have cartouches.

Pop Culture Shoutout:

In *The Prince of Egypt*, Moses wears a pendant with his name in a cartouche. It's not just jewelry—it's identity, history, and divine connection all wrapped into one glyph-stamped oval.

Who Got a Cartouche?

Only the most elite. Pharaohs, queens, and sometimes gods or deified royals. Regular folks? Nope. No cartouche for you unless you earned it.

Cleopatra's name was often written in a cartouche—so were the Ptolemies. In fact, her cartouche helped scholars crack parts of the Rosetta Stone because her name appeared in both Greek and hieroglyphic scripts.

The Royal Five: Pharaoh's Titles

Each pharaoh had not one but five royal names, kind of like a superhero with multiple identities. Each came with a title and symbolic meaning. Here they are:

1. Horus Name – Links the pharaoh with the god Horus (falcon-headed protector).
2. Nebty Name – "Two Ladies" name (Wadjet and Nekhbet goddesses).
3. Golden Horus Name – Symbol of eternal rule and divine power.
4. Throne Name – The official regnal name, written in a cartouche.
5. Birth Name – Given at birth, also written in a cartouche.

The last two were the ones you'd most commonly see—and learn to write. We'll focus on those!

How to Write a Cartouche

Let's try building one together. Take the name Tutankhamun, one of the most famous pharaohs ever.

Break it into its phonetic elements: T – W – T – ' – N – K – Ḥ – I – M – N

Now find the corresponding uniliteral and biliteral glyphs from earlier chapters. Place them vertically or horizontally, then draw the oval cartouche around them. Add a straight line at the base. Voilà—royalty!

Doodling Challenge:

Write *your own name* in a cartouche using uniliterals and determinatives. Design your oval. Maybe add decorative flair—papyrus leaves, ankh symbols, scarabs. Go full royal mode.

Nicknames, Pet Names, and Titles

Ancient Egyptians also loved titles. They described professions, achievements, or social rank. You'd often see:

- "Scribe of the Divine Scrolls"
- "Overseer of Granaries"
- "Wife of the High Priest"
- "Fan Bearer on the Right of the King" (real job title—look it up!)

You can make your own:

"Savior of Snacks," "Doodler of Destiny," "Guardian of the Wi-Fi Scrolls."

Yes, it's silly. But it's also exactly how many Egyptian titles worked. They were literal, poetic, and sometimes a little dramatic.

Creative Project: The Cartouche Wall

Design a wall of cartouches for:

- Yourself
- Your family or friend group
- Your favorite pop culture characters

Write their names using glyphs. Add titles. Arrange them like a Pharaoh's temple relief.

Example:

- Batman = "Dark Protector of the City"
- Spider-Man = "Weaver of Webs, Bringer of Justice"
- Daenerys = "Mother of Dragons, Breaker of Chains"
  (Use glyphs for "mother," "fire," "freedom," etc.)

  Optional: Print and color your cartouches or turn them into bookmarks or stickers.

Coming Up Next…

You've got a name, a title, and a sense of layout—now let's expand your hieroglyphic vocabulary! In Chapter 14, we'll dive into common words and phrases: blessings, greetings, famous quotes, and everyday terms from the ancient world. By then, you'll be writing simple sentences like a seasoned scribe.

Until then, wear your cartouche with pride—and keep doodling with purpose!

Chapter 14: Common Words and Phrases

Say What? Speaking Ancient Egyptian in Style

Now that you can spell names, stack glyphs like a champ, and wrap your identity in a majestic cartouche, it's time to learn how the ancient Egyptians actually spoke and wrote to one another.

Hieroglyphs weren't just used to carve royal proclamations—they were used to express affection, ask for blessings, and even tell jokes (yes, they had jokes!). In this chapter, we'll break down the most useful and frequent words and phrases that show up in ancient texts.

Pop Culture Moment:

If you've ever shouted "Wakanda Forever!" or whispered "May the Force be with you," you already get how powerful a recurring phrase can be. Egyptians had their own versions—and now you're going to learn them.

Greetings and Blessings

Ancient Egyptians weren't big on "Hi" or "Hello" like we are, but they had formulas to show respect, give blessings, and wish people well. These greetings often appear in letters, tomb inscriptions, and offerings.

Common Phrases:

☥ ⚱ 🗊 — ankh, wedja, seneb

Meaning: "Life, prosperity, and health"

- ☥ *(ankh)* – Life

- ⚱ *(wedja)* – Prosperity or well-being

- 🗊 *(seneb)* – Health

    This is the classic Egyptian blessing—often found in temple inscriptions and personal prayers. Think of it like "Live long and prosper" in the ancient world.

⚖☥ — **di ankh**

Meaning: "Gives life"

- ⚖ (*di*) – To give (han
- ☥ (*ankh*) – Life
  Commonly used when referring to gods or kings granting blessings or vitality.

◡ — **neb**

Meaning: "Lord" or "Master"

- ◡ (*neb*) – Basket or throne symbol
  Appears frequently in royal titles like "Lord of the Two Lands" (*neb tawy*).

Frequently Used Words

Concepts in Hieroglyphs (Text Format)

English: Life
Egyptian Sound: Ankh

Glyph: ☥

Glyph Description: ⚲ (looks like a cross with loop, but actually a sandal tie)

English: Power/Strength
Egyptian Sound: Djed

Glyph: 𓊽
Glyph Description: Column-like backbone

English: Peace
Egyptian Sound: Hetep

Glyph: ⌐△⌐
Glyph Description: Offering table with loaf

English: Love
Egyptian Sound: Mer

Glyph: 𓌉〰
Glyph Description: Hoe and water ripple

English: Truth
Egyptian Sound: Ma'at

Glyph: 𓆄𓏏𓁐
Glyph Description: Feather + seated goddess

English: King
Egyptian Sound: Nswt

Glyph: 〰𓇋𓏏 or also written quite commonly as 𓏏𓇯〰 but pronounced the same.
Glyph Description: Crowned man with crook

English: God
Egyptian Sound: Ntr

Glyph: ⌐
Glyph Description: Flag or axe on a pole

English: Woman
Egyptian Sound: Hmt

Glyphs: 𓇋𓏏
Extra Optional Glyph Determmantive: Seated woman

English: Son
Egyptian Sound: Sa

Glyph: ⟋

Optional Glyph Determantive: Child or seated boy

English: Eye
Egyptian Sound: Irt

Glyph: 𓂀

Glyph Description: Eye (like Eye of Horus   )

These words make up the foundation of Egyptian communication—and they often came with symbolic power. Saying "ankh" wasn't just about *life*, it was about wishing life into existence.

Fun Fact:

The phrase "ankh djed hetep" (life, stability, peace) was commonly used in temple inscriptions. It was like their version of a motto or creed—think "Liberty, Equality, Fraternity," but with a way cooler font.

☥ 𓊽 ⌂ — **ankh, djed, hetep**

Translation: "Life, stability, peace"

☥   Life

⌂   Peace, offe

Hieroglyphic Poetry (Yes, Really)

Egyptians were big on poetic phrasing, especially in tombs and romantic inscriptions.

Sample Phrase:

"May your ka live forever."
→ *ankh ka djet*

- *ankh* = life
- *ka* = soul/essence
- *djet* = eternity (often shown as a snake)

It's a way of saying "May your soul be eternal"—and it's deeply personal, almost spiritual.

⚰ ⊔ ⚱ — **ankh ka djet**

Translation: "May your ka live forever."

Glyph	Transliteration	Meaning
⊔		Spiritual essence or life-force

This was a **standard funerary blessing** in Ancient Egypt, invoking eternal life for a person's *ka*—their divine life-force. It appears frequently in tomb inscriptions and on statues.

Modern Analogy:

It's like writing "Rest in Power" or "Forever in our hearts" on a memorial plaque. Beautiful, respectful, and symbolic.

Practice Time: Create Your Own Offering

Try composing a short offering phrase using these common words. For example:

"An offering that the king gives: life, peace, and prosperity."
→ *di nswt hetep: ankh, wedja, seneb*

Now add your glyphs:

- Hand (di)
- Crowned man (nswt)
- Offering table (hetep)
- Symbols for life, prosperity, health (⚰, plant, human)

Arrange them like a temple inscription—with symmetry, balance, and a little flair.

Design Tip:

Frame your phrase in a decorative border. Add small gods or sacred animals watching over it. You're not just learning a phrase—you're building an ancient art piece.

Make It Modern: Hieroglyphic Affirmations

Try turning these into daily affirmations or Instagram-worthy mantras:

- "I am Ma'at." (I speak truth and balance.)
- "I walk with Ankh." (I carry life and energy.)
- HIERATIC"My Ka is strong." (My essence is unshakable.)

Write them in English, then translate them into glyphs using your uniliteral and biliteral knowledge. Decorate. Stylize. Maybe even tattoo one if you're bold like that.

Coming Up Next...

You're fluent in blessings, titles, and truths—so now it's time to talk numbers and dates! In Chapter 15 we'll explore how Egyptians counted, wrote large numbers, and tracked time using lunar cycles, calendars, and festival days.

Math + magic + scribal doodles = the next step in your journey.

Until then, may you walk in balance—and keep doodling with purpose.

Chapter 15: Numbers and Dates

Math, Magic, and Moon Phases

Ancient Egyptians weren't just great artists and builders—they were also pretty impressive mathematicians. From measuring land after the Nile's floods to calculating the stars, they needed a way to count, keep time, and record important events.
And guess what? They did it all with hieroglyphs.

Pop Culture Moment:

Ever notice how in *Moon Knight*, Egyptian symbols are used to track celestial alignments and ancient rituals? That's not fantasy—it's actually pretty close to how Egyptians used calendars, astronomy, and numbers to shape their world.

How Egyptian Numbers Worked

Unlike our 1–10 place value system, Egyptians used additive numerals—meaning they wrote out numbers by repeating symbols.

Number Glyphs:

1   Single stroke

100,000   Frog (fertility, abundance)

Quick Math Lesson:

Want to write 3,245? Stack these glyphs:
- 3 lotus flowers (3,000)
- 2 coils of rope (200)
- 4 heel bones (40)
- 5 strokes (5)

It's like tally marks on steroids—beautiful, symbolic, and surprisingly precise.

No Zero, No Problem

The Egyptians didn't have a zero. But they didn't really need one—their number system was all about presence, not absence. If something wasn't there, they just didn't write it.

Design Tip:

Think of each number as an illustration. Writing 27, for example, is like making a piece of number art: 2 heel bones + 7 strokes. It's visual math, and it looks great on papyrus.

Egyptian Timekeeping: The Sacred Calendar

The Egyptian year was divided into three seasons, each reflecting the rhythm of the Nile:

1. Akhet (𓆼𓏏) – "Inundation"

- **Glyphs:**
  - 𓆼 (*ḫ*) – Horizon or flood symbol
  - 𓏏 (*t*) – Feminine ending
- **Time of Year:** June–October
- **Meaning:** The season of the Nile flood, symbolizing renewal and fertility.

2. Peret (𓊪𓂋𓏏) – "Emergence"

- **Glyphs:**
  - 𓊪 (*p*) – Stool or Mat
  - 𓂋 I – Mouth
  - 𓏏 (*t*) – Feminine ending
- **Time of Year:** October–February
- **Meaning:** The growing season when crops sprout from the freshly deposited silt.

3. Shemu (𓈙𓅓𓅱) – "Harvest"

- **Glyphs:**
  - 𓈙 (*š*) – Pool
  - 𓅓 (*m*) – Owl
  - 𓅱 (*w*) – Quail chick
- **Time of Year:** February–June
- **Meaning:** The dry season and time for harvest, associated with reaping and storage.

Each season had four months, and each month had 30 days. That's 360 days. To make up the extra 5 days in a solar year, they added five "epagomenal" days—bonus festival days for the gods' birthdays.

Mythical Note:

Those extra five days were said to be when gods like Osiris, Isis, and Horus were born. So yes, they literally wrote divine birthdays into their calendar.

How Dates Were Written

Dates were often tied to the reign of a pharaoh, like saying:
"Year 4, Month 2 of Akhet, Day 15 of the reign of Thutmose III."
It looked something like:
- Hieroglyph for "Year"
- Number glyphs
- Season glyph (Akhet = water lines + papyrus)
- Month and day glyphs
- Name of the ruling pharaoh (inside a cartouche)

Star Wars Analogy:

It's like saying, "5 BBY (Before Battle of Yavin)" or "Year 3 of the Mandalorian." They tracked time based on leaders and epic events.

Moon Phases and Festivals

The Egyptian calendar also tied into lunar cycles and star risings—especially the star Sirius (Sopdet), which heralded the Nile's flood. This wasn't just science—it was spiritual. Celestial events triggered festivals, rituals, and agricultural shifts.

Major Calendar Moments:
- Wepet Renpet – New Year festival, tied to Sirius
- Opet Festival – Celebrating Amun, Mut, and Khonsu
- Sed Festival – A royal jubilee to refresh the pharaoh's power

Modern Analogy:

Think of these like a mix of New Year's Eve, Comic-Con, and a presidential inauguration—all rolled into one, but carved into stone and tied to stargazing.

Practice Time: Record an Ancient Birthday

Try writing your own birthday as if you were an Egyptian scribe.

Let's say:
- You were born in Year 7 of Pharaoh Beyoncé I

- On Day 12 of the second month of Peret

You'd write:
- "Year 7, Month 2 of Peret, Day 12 of the reign of Beyoncé (in cartouche)"

Stack your number glyphs, season symbol, and her royal name glyphs inside a cartouche. Yes, this is the coolest historical fan art ever.

How Plurals Work in Hieroglyphs

In ancient Egyptian, plurals aren't formed by adding an "s" like in English. Instead, the Egyptians used **visual repetition** and clever glyph additions. One of the most common markers is the **quail chick** (transliterated as *w*), placed at the end of a word to indicate **plural**. But it doesn't stop there—scribes would also sometimes **repeat the final determinative** (the symbol that shows a word's category) **two or even three times** to signal "many."

For example, to write "mountains" or "foreign lands," you might see a triple hill glyph like this:

ᴍᴍᴍ

This visual stacking isn't just decorative—it reinforces meaning. A single glyph shows *one*, two indicates *pair*, and **three or more** glyphs means *many*. Egyptians loved symbolism, and plurals were often about rhythm, form, and emphasis—not just grammar.

Creative Challenge: Build a Sacred Calendar

Design a one-page Egyptian calendar that includes:
- Three seasons
- Glyph-based month names
- Major "festivals" you create (like "Feast of the Cat Scroll" or "Day of the Meme")
- Your friends' birthdays in pharaonic style

Color-code it, frame it, and hang it next to your modern calendar. It's time travel… in doodle form.

Coming Up Next…

Now that you've mastered words, names, and even time itself, you're ready for visual vocabulary. In Chapter 16, we'll explore how to draw and use hieroglyphs for everyday life—objects, animals, nature, family, and more.

Soon, you'll be labeling your sketchbook, organizing your room, or decorating your journal—all in hieroglyphs.

Until then, stay timeless—and keep doodling with purpose.

Chapter 16: Everyday Objects and Concepts in Hieroglyphs

Hieroglyphs for Your Real Life (and Your Doodles)

Up to this point, you've learned how to write names, build phrases, count like a scribe, and bless someone with eternal life. Pretty impressive. Now let's get practical—because the ancient Egyptians didn't just write about kings and gods. They wrote about their daily lives, too.

From what they ate and wore to what animals they raised and where they lived, the Egyptians turned *everything* into a glyph. And once you learn these symbols, you can start labeling your own world, ancient-style.

Pop Culture Lens:

Imagine an Egyptian version of *The Sims* or *Animal Crossing*, where instead of selecting items from a menu, you tap hieroglyphs for "bed," "cat," or "banana." That's the vibe of this chapter. You're building your own world—in pictures and glyphs.

Family and People

Let's start with people, because Egyptians were very into who's who in the household.

Concept	Glyph Description
Son	Same as "child," context-dependent

rsonal and Family Terms

:ept	Sound	Glyph Description
ın	Z	Seatied man
nan	Hmt	Seatied woman Cieler to mout
ild	Hrd	Seatied child Finger to mouth
ın	Sa	Same as 'child, context-dep
;hter	Sat	Slemelas child feminine ending
her	Mut	Seated woman +extra reed/or arm
ner	It	Sected man extra reed/arm

These glyphs were used in everything from tomb inscriptions to love poetry to family trees. In other words: the original ancestry.com.

Try This:

Write your family members' names in hieroglyphs, then label each with the correct glyph (mom, dad, brother, sister, etc.). You've just made a Pharaoh-level family tree.

Animals

The Egyptians were obsessed with animals—not just as pets, but as gods, guardians, and metaphors.

Animal	Glyph Description
Cow	Cow with horns
Crocodile	Sobek the croc

Cool Fact:

The word "miw" for cat has shown up on tomb walls *with real cat illustrations*—like early comic captions. Egyptians loved their cats just as much as the Internet does. Also, note the name of a cat in Egyptian is the very sound that they make!~ Try sounding it out to see what we mean.

Nature & Environment

Here's how the ancients captured their surroundings:

Water   Zigzag ripple

Desert   Red land dunes

Concept	Sound	Glyph Description
Tree	nht	Palm or tree shape
Water	mw	Zigzag ripple
Sky	ra	Sircle with sun
Earth	ta	Sky bar with sun
Desert	dsrt	Red land dunes
Mountain	ḳā	Triple mountain glyph

Try This:

Draw a landscape in Egyptian style: put the earth on the bottom, mountains above it, sun in the sky, and trees between. Use actual glyphs to label everything like an illustrated scroll.

Food & Drink

What's for dinner in 1200 BCE?

Beer   hnqt   ·ith handle

/Drink	Sound	Glyph Description
·ead	*t*	△
·eer	*hnqt*	🏺
·leat	*ha*	🐆
·ater	*mw*	〰〰〰
·ruit	*nbs*	○○ ○○ Clusters (dates, figs)

These show up often in offering scenes, where people provide food for gods or the dead to enjoy in the afterlife.

Hieroglyphic Menu:

Create a menu for a fictional ancient Egyptian dinner party:
- "Bread, beer, beef, figs, and honey."
  Write each item with glyphs and draw your own dish icons

Tools, Clothing & Objects

House   Rectangle with doorwa·

Sandals   Foot + strap

A "house" glyph (pr) appears in so many names and places, like "Per-Ra" (House of Ra). It's a building block—literally.

Object	Sound	Hierogly
House	pr	
Staff	wʌs	
Mirror	ḫât	
Clothing	špst	
Sandals	sḵ	
Boat	dpt	

Design Exercise:

Draw your room as a floorplan with Egyptian glyphs labeling items like bed (nht), mirror (ḫʻt), and door (prt). Ancient IKEA, anyone?

Build Your World with Glyphs

Combine what you've learned from this chapter and create your own glyph-labeled micro world:
- Your room
- Your pet collection
- A garden with plants and animals
- Your ideal pharaoh-approved wardrobe

Add glyphs and names for each object, and maybe a short sentence or offering phrase ("The cat rests in the house under Ra.")

Bonus: Write your grocery list in hieroglyphs and show it off like a scribal flex.

Coming Up Next...

Now that you're fluent in real-world glyphs, you're ready for the deep end. In Chapter 14, we'll practice translating real inscriptions—from tomb walls to temple carvings. We'll take what you've learned and read it in the wild, decoding ancient texts like a boss.
Soon, you'll go from doodler to decoder.

Until then, label your life—and keep doodling with purpose!

Chapter 17: Translating Real Inscriptions

From Doodles to Decoding

You've mastered letters, sounds, phrases, and even the layout. Now it's time to step up and do what scribes did: read the real thing.

Don't panic. Ancient inscriptions might *look* intimidating, but remember: they're just fancy, stylized pictures spelling out thoughts, feelings, prayers, and facts. Like if emoji, calligraphy, and graphic design had a baby.

In this chapter, you'll learn how to break down inscriptions step-by-step and translate them. Whether it's a tomb blessing, a temple dedication, or a name scrawled by a worker on a stone, the structure is surprisingly consistent—and we've got the tools now.

Real World Setup:

Imagine standing in the Valley of the Kings, running your fingers over a faded glyph: a falcon, a reed, an ankh. You realize... it says "Ra gives life." Boom. You just read something written 3,000 years ago.

Step 1: Spot the Cartouche

Start with the easy win. If you see a cartouche (oval with glyphs inside), that's likely a royal name.

Let's say the glyphs inside include:

- ⊙ (Sun disk) = Ra

- ꡡ (Cobra) = Djed or Djr

- ⌒ (Hand) = Di ("to give")You're likely looking at: Ra-di → "Given by Ra" or "Gift of Ra" (common part of names like Ramesses = Ra-mses)

Hollywood Tip:

Cartouches in movies like *The Mummy* or *Stargate* usually carry a Pharaoh's throne name. In real life, decoding one often gives you the full ID of who's being honored—or cursed, depending on the text.

Step 2: Identify the Sentence Flow

Remember from Chapter 5: Verb–Subject–Object is the standard flow. Look for the action glyph (like "give," "speak," "praise") first.

For example:

- ⌐ (Hand) = "di" = give

- ⚬ ⌀ (Crowned seated figure) = "nswt" = king
- ⚬ ☥ (Ankh) = lifedi nswt ankh = "The king gives life"

Pro Scribe Tip:

Even if the visual order seems flipped, sacred conventions (like honorific transposition) may place gods' names before verbs or objects, but the grammar underneath follows the classic pattern.

Step 3: Look for Repetition and Patterns

Ancient Egyptian was formulaic—kind of like liturgical Latin or Shakespearean English. Certain phrases appear over and over:

Common Templates:
4. ***"An offering that the king gives…"***
   → *ḥtp dỉ nsw*

   Hieroglyphs: ⚊⚬▢ ⚊⎮〰⚊⚲

5. ***"Life, prosperity, and health…"***
   → *ꜥnḫ, wḏ³, snb*

   Hieroglyphs: ☥ ⬭⬯ ⎮〰⚲

6. ***"The good god…"***
   → *nṯr nfr*

   Hieroglyphs: ⎮⚭

Once you recognize these, the rest of the sentence often just fills in who's doing what to whom.

Example In Context:

On a stele, you might read: ⚊⚬ ⌀ ☥ ⚬ 𓀀 = "The king gives life and bread to the person (named below)"
Boom. You just read a line from someone's offering table.

Step 4: Use Determinatives to Clarify Meaning

When you see a glyph followed by a symbol like:
- • = person
- • = place
- • = action

It helps you know whether you're reading a name, a city, a verb, or an object. If you're stuck on a sound, use the determinative like a genre tag for the word.

Step 5: Work It Backwards (if needed)

Sometimes inscriptions are damaged or out of order. When that happens, work backwards from what you *do* know:
- Found a cartouche? Identify the Pharaoh.
- Recognize "ankh wedja seneb"? That's your blessing.
- Saw "di nswt"? You know it's an offering phrase.

Use the pieces like puzzle parts and reconstruct what's missing. That's what real Egyptologists do!

Decode Challenge:

Here's a line from an offering:
Your task: Translate it using what you know.
- "The king gives life, grain, bread, and beer…"
  → a very complete offering!

Practice Exercise: Decode This Tomb Phrase

♀   **(Emojis, just for fun)**

(Hieroglyphs)

di nswt ankh irt djd ḥwt rmt **(Transliteration)**

Hints:
- Start with the verb
- Look for nouns with determinatives
- Use glyph groups you already know

Want to verify? Translation:

"The king gives life and protection to the person in the house (temple)."

Here are the words broken up:

King ( )

ankh

⟋⟍ ⟋⟍   ꞏnake / defens

rmṯ (per: Man/people (   )

Creative Project: Make Your Own Inscription

Using glyphs, draw and translate a:
- Temple wall dedication
- Tomb phrase honoring someone
- Offering scene for a fictional Pharaoh

Make it beautiful. Group your glyphs into balanced blocks. Add determinatives. Draw gods or animals along the borders. And be sure to include a cartouche or two.

Optional Bonus:

Create a frameable "glyph quote" like:
7. **"Truth is balance."**
   → *M³ꜥt ḥtp*

   Hieroglyphs: 𓂝 △ ⬚
   (*M³ꜥt* = Ma'at / truth, *ḥtp* = balance, peace, offering)

Coming Up Next…

You've now crossed into full translation territory! In Chapter 18, we'll zoom out and explore the symbolism and sacred meaning behind hieroglyphs—why a vulture meant power, or a feather meant justice. These weren't just letters—they were loaded icons.

Understanding their spiritual and cultural power adds a whole new layer to your doodling and decoding.

Until then, keep reading the stones—and keep doodling with purpose!

Chapter 18: Symbolism and Sacred Meaning

When Every Glyph Is a Spell

If you've been thinking of hieroglyphs as just letters with fancy edges—think again. In ancient Egypt, writing was sacred. Glyphs weren't merely tools for communication; they were acts of creation. To write something was to *make it real.*
That's why the ancient Egyptian word for writing, *medu netjer*, means "words of the gods."
So, when you doodle a hieroglyph, you're not just practicing a symbol—you're engaging with a whole worldview. It's like drawing a rune, a sigil, or a magical emblem. And the Egyptians knew it.

Pop Culture Vibe:

Think of Doctor Strange drawing symbols in the air or the spells in *Harry Potter* that have specific motion and intent. That's how hieroglyphs worked. They were visual spells.

The Power Behind the Pictures

Let's break down the symbolic layers behind some common glyphs you've already learned:

	Djed / Djd	Snake – Protection, rebirth, danger
	Scarab	Kheper – Becoming, transformation, rebirth

Deep Dive:

The *ankh* wasn't just a symbol for "life." It was believed to hold life. That's why gods are often shown handing it to pharaohs or placing it under their noses—like a divine oxygen mask.

Animals Weren't Just Animals

Animal glyphs were avatars of gods or cosmic forces:
- Falcon (Horus): Vision, protection, sky power
- Ibis (Thoth): Wisdom, writing, moon cycles
- Cat (Bastet): Grace, protection, motherhood

- Crocodile (Sobek): Power, fertility, chaos
- Jackal (Anubis): Death, protection of the dead

ɔh		Deity	Symbolism
			Vision, protection, sky power
		Thoth	Wisdom, writing, moon cycles
		Bastet	Grace, protection, motherhood
		Sobek	Power, fertility, chaos
		Anubis	Death, protection

Modern Translation:

If you picked an animal as your spirit guide, the Egyptians would *absolutely* turn it into a glyph and link it to a divine trait. It's like a celestial Pokémon system—each one with attributes, powers, and mythic backstories.

Color and Style Meant Something Too

We haven't talked much about color, but when hieroglyphs were painted, colors held power too:
Colors in Egyptian Symbolism with Hieroglyphs

Green (w3ḏ)   h, life, regeneration *(Osiris)*

Yellow/Gold (nbw)   ɔy, sun, eternity *(Ra, gods' skin)*

Black (km)   and rebirth *(Anubis, Nile silt = fertility)*

Try This:

Redraw your favorite glyphs using color. Make your scarab green, your sun gold, your feather white or blue. You're not just coloring—you're activating symbolic meaning.

Hieroglyphs as Magic in Real Rituals

In tombs, temples, and scrolls, hieroglyphs were used in:
- Spells from the *Book of the Dead*
- Protective amulets
- Funerary inscriptions to guide the dead
- Temple walls to glorify the gods and ensure balance in the universe

They believed that as long as something was written, it existed eternally. That's why scribes carved names so carefully—erasing a name could "kill" someone's spirit.

Big Idea:

Writing = memory = eternity. That's why Pharaohs had their names plastered everywhere. And that's why you putting *your name* in a cartouche is more powerful than you thought.

Write with Meaning

Now that you know these deeper meanings, go back to your favorite inscriptions or glyphs and ask:
- What does this say *about the person*?
- Is the animal a god reference?
- Why use that word order or symbol?
- What's the emotional or spiritual tone?

Creative Practice:

Write a short affirmation, quote, or wish using glyphs and color them with symbolic meanings:
- "Rise again" with a green scarab and blue sun
- "Speak truth" with a feather and mouth
- "Walk in balance" with two legs and Ma'at's feather

Final Creative Challenge: Design a Glyph Shrine

Create an illustrated panel using 3–5 hieroglyphs that mean something personal to you:
- Your spirit animal
- A word you live by (truth, strength, love)
- A visual metaphor for your dream or identity

Use layout balance (Chapter 6), glyph accuracy, and symbolic color. Turn it into a bookmark, journal cover, tattoo idea, or wall art.

Bonus: Add offering hands or rays from the sun to "activate" the image with sacred power.

Coming Up Next...

You've made it through the most sacred layers of glyph language! In Chapter 19, we'll return to the doodling desk and get creative with how to draw, stylize, and expand your own glyphs. We'll turn learning into art journaling—how to use hieroglyphs for sketchbooks, class notes, visual diaries, or even comics.

Until then, remember: every line you draw *means* something.

Keep creating—and keep doodling with purpose.

Chapter 19: Hieroglyphs as Doodles

The Art of Drawing History

Let's be real: learning to read and write ancient Egyptian isn't just academic—it's *aesthetic*. These aren't just letters, they're drawings. Each hieroglyph is part of a massive cultural sketchbook, and now that you know how they work, you can use them not just to communicate but to create.

This chapter is all about bringing hieroglyphs into your modern life through art journaling, sketching, and personal expression.

Pop Culture Twist:

Think of this chapter as your glyph version of bullet journaling, anime sketching, or tattoo designing. We're not doing homework—we're crafting something timeless and personal.

Why Doodling Works

The human brain learns better through drawing. That's not woo-woo—that's neuroscience. Drawing activates memory, spatial reasoning, and even emotional connection. That's exactly how the Egyptians *taught* scribes: they didn't just copy letters—they illustrated stories.

So when you doodle hieroglyphs, you're:
- Reinforcing language learning
- Connecting emotionally with ideas
- Practicing mindfulness
- Participating in 5,000-year-old visual culture

Think of this like Egyptian calligraphy—but with a flair for the artistic.

Sketching Hieroglyphs with Style

Start with the uniliterals and biliterals you know. But instead of copying them perfectly, play with them:
- Exaggerate the curves of the cobra
- Add feather texture to Ma'at's glyph
- Turn the reed into a stylized pen
- Give your cartouche decorative wings or vines

Remember: Egyptian scribes were *designers*. They arranged glyphs not just for readability, but for balance and beauty.

Art Prompts Using Glyphs

Here are some fun and creative ways to incorporate hieroglyphs into your sketchbook or journal:
8. Glyph of the Day
Pick one glyph each day and:
- Practice drawing it 3–5 times

- Write a short sentence using it
- Draw a scene or metaphor using it

Example: "Snake" = protection + danger

Draw a glyph-based comic panel: snake coiled around a temple gate = guardian spirit

9. Emotional Glyph Journal

Create a mood tracker using glyphs:
Emotion-Based Hieroglyph Interpretations

☥ (Ankh)   Energized

🪲 (Scarab)   In transition

▭ (Door E   Excited or stressed

Color-code them and use them to track your week like emoji meets ancient sacred art.

10. Glyph Comics

Draw a 3-panel mini comic using only glyphs:
- Frame 1: Cartouche with a name
- Frame 2: Action glyph + object (verb + object)
- Frame 3: Offering scene or conclusion (life, peace, etc.)

Think of it as *emoji storytelling meets Rosetta Stone fan art.*

11. Dream Glyph Mapping

After a dream or big idea, try representing it entirely in glyphs:
- A journey = walking legs
- A mystery = star + eye
- A conflict = two animals facing off

Use spacing and balance to tell the story visually—like a sacred storyboard.

12. Design Your Own Glyph

Once you've mastered the classics, design a modern hieroglyph:
- A phone = sound + communication
- A heart with wings = freedom + love

- A planet with lines = travel, space

Give it a name, assign a sound, and explain what it means. That's exactly what ancient scribes did when creating signs for new ideas.

From Notebook to Temple (Almost)

Once your sketchbook is filled with glyphs:
- Try turning your designs into posters or prints
- Design your own "papyrus scroll" page
- Create stickers, bookmarks, or journal covers
- Even try writing your name and title on a stone or wood plaque!

Modern Meets Ancient Tip:

Use parchment-style paper, gold pens, or watercolor washes to give your glyph doodles an aged, mysterious feel.

Final Creative Challenge: Make a Visual Glyph Diary Page
1. Pick a word to reflect your day or week (strength, rebirth, chaos, love)
2. Find 3–5 glyphs that symbolize it
3. Arrange them into a balanced visual piece
4. Add a cartouche with your name and the date (Egyptian-style)
5. Decorate with sacred elements—sun disk, feathers, stars, scarabs, etc.

You've just created art *and* recorded history. Pharaohs would be jealous.

Coming Up Next…
You've officially unlocked the artist-scribe within. In Chapter 20, we'll explore how the Hieroglyphic language is a truly Egyptian invention and how you need to have an Egyptian Mind sometimes to understand it!

Until then, open your sketchbook, sharpen your stylus—and keep doodling with purpose.

Chapter 20: You Need an Egyptian Mind

So, you're getting pretty good at this hieroglyph thing. You can spot an ankh from a mile away, recognize a seated man when you see one, and maybe even sketch a respectable-looking scarab. But here's the truth:

To *really* understand hieroglyphs, you have to think like an **ancient Egyptian**.

You need an **Egyptian mind**.

What Does That Even Mean?

It means ditching your modern assumptions. Stop thinking in pixels and paper. Forget that you've ever seen a typewriter or a Times New Roman font.

Because hieroglyphs weren't written for *you*. They were written by Egyptians, for Egyptians—people whose **entire worldview** was shaped by **the Nile, the desert, the sun, and the sacred order of nature**.

They wrote what they **saw**. What they **knew**. What they **lived**.

That's why to decode their language, you need to understand their environment—their daily tools, their animals, their architecture, even their shoelaces (we'll get to that).

Wait… That's Not a Feather?!

Let's talk about one of the most famous cases of mistaken glyph identity: the **reed leaf**.

For decades, scholars studying Egyptian writing from afar assumed that the glyph ⟨ was a **feather**. It looked like one, after all. A long, thin, tapering shape—clearly the stylus of some divine bird, right?

Wrong.

Enter **Jean-François Champollion**, the French linguistic detective who cracked the code of hieroglyphs in the 1820s. When he finally made it to **Egypt**, something clicked. He saw the **actual Nile reeds** growing along the riverbanks—tall, slender plants used for everything from writing tools to basket weaving. And just like that, the mystery feather became what it truly was:

A reed.

Champollion realized something critical: to understand the glyphs, you had to be **in Egypt**. You had to breathe the hot Nile air, stand among the reeds, look at the same sun glinting off the same temple stones.

Nile papyrus reed and its hieroglyph form.

You had to have an **Egyptian mind**.

Everything Is Egyptian

Every glyph is a **snapshot of Egyptian life**. Let's walk through just a few of the hundreds:

- ⚱ – Twisted flax (used to tie sandals and wrap bodies)

- ⌑ – Floor plan of a house or shrine

- ⌇ – Folded cloth (every household had one)

- ⌒ – Horned viper (common in Egypt, dangerous, yes, but sacred too)

- ⊏o – A jug and a grain scoop for **beer**—not a party drink, but a **daily staple**

- ⌒ – A folded bolt of fabric and a loaf = "st" for place or temple

- ⌂ – An **offering table** with a loaf of bread

- ⌒ – A **loaf**—just that. Bread was currency, ritual, life itself.

And then there's the **ankh**: ☥. Sure, it means "life." But what is it *really*? Scholars now know it represents a **sandal strap**. Yes—like the loop and crosspiece you'd use to tie on your flip-flops in the Egyptian sand.

So, yes, your symbol of eternal life started as... **a shoelace**.

Beware the power of my shoelace! (tell that to someone with an ankh tattoo…)

Egyptian Glyphs Are Rooted in *Egypt*

This is why hieroglyphs can't be separated from Egypt itself. They're visual language born from:

- The **Nile** and its sacred flooding cycles
- The **animals** Egyptians lived with and worshipped
- The **tools** of their labor
- The **rituals** of death, birth, and offering
- The **structures** they built and lived in
- And the **values** they held sacred

You're not reading a **code**. You're reading a **culture**.

The Takeaway: You're Not Just Learning Symbols

You're learning how an entire civilization **saw the world**.

That's why your Western, modern, emoji-trained brain sometimes stumbles. Because this language isn't alphabetic in the way we're used to. It's **embodied**. Each glyph is not just a sound—it's a **real thing**, pulled from Egyptian life and infused with meaning.

So as you study these glyphs, ask yourself:

- What *is* this a picture of?
- What did this mean to an Egyptian?
- Where would they see this? Use it? Revere it?

The more you think like an ancient Egyptian, the more the glyphs will start to speak to you—not just with their sounds, but with their soul.

And that, my friend, is when your doodling becomes something more.

It becomes **doodling with purpose**.

Chapter 21: The Weird Exceptions — King, Osiris, and Beer

By now, you've probably gotten the hang of Egyptian writing. It's logical. It's beautifully structured. One symbol = one sound (usually). Determinatives tell you what kind of word it is. Cartouches wrap royal names. Everything fits.

Except when it doesn't.

Welcome to the land of linguistic exceptions—where sacred words, powerful names, and ancient traditions bend the rules and expect you to just go with it. This is the chapter where you'll meet three of the strangest and most rule-breaking hieroglyphic words in the game:

-  **(nswt) = King**
-  **(wsjr) = Osiris**
-  **(hnqt) = Beer**

Let's decode the mystery.

"King" –  – *nswt*

On the surface, this should be simple. The word for "king" is **nswt**.

But here's the twist: it's not pronounced anything like how it looks in English. For starters, there's **no vowel** between the "s" and the "w" in the script, so you'd think it sounds like "nswt" as written. But linguistically, it's more like "nesut."

Now the kicker: the "t" at the end, which normally marks **feminine words**, is included in "king," a **masculine** title. Huh?

That's because "nswt" refers not to the man himself, but to the **institution** of kingship—like "the Crown" or "the Throne." In that sense, it's grammatically feminine. So yes, the king's title ends in a feminine "t"—because he's repping the abstract power of the throne, not just flexing with a crook and flail.

Mind. Blown.

"Osiris" –  – *wsjr*

Now let's talk **Osiris**—the god of the dead, rebirth, and one seriously goth underworld. In hieroglyphs, his name appears as  (transliterated as *wsjr*).

But here's where it gets weird: Osiris's name breaks the usual rules for how words are built. For one thing, it begins with the **god determinative** ()—which usually goes at the **end** of a word. Not here. He leads with it.

That's kind of like starting someone's name with "   " because they're *that* divine.

Also, the spelling includes ⌐ (a kind of throne or seat) and ⌐ (mouth or "r"), but the pronunciation we get from later Coptic and Greek traditions—"Osiris"—doesn't quite match what the glyphs say. It's likely closer to *Asar* or *Wesir* in ancient Egyptian. But the Greeks Hellenized it, and now we've got "Osiris."

Think of it like a mythological rebrand. Ancient gods: they're just like us—except immortal and spell-checked by priests.

"Beer" ▬ ⌐o – *hnqt*

You'd think a nation built around bread and beer would have a straightforward glyph for "beer," right?

Nope.

⌐o (hnqt) is one of the most unexpected spellings in Egyptian. First off, the glyphs used are a **liquid jug with a handle** and a **grain-like measure**—suggesting volume and storage more than drinkability. There's no cute barley glyph or "cheers" sign here. Instead, it's written almost like a **ration measurement** or **commodity**, because that's exactly what beer was: a staple foodstuff, an offering, and even *currency*.

So while we might expect a bubbly mug or a " " emoji equivalent, the Egyptians saw beer more like an asset—a resource to manage, distribute, and record. Which is exactly why the glyphs for **hnqt** look like they came from an accountant's notebook.

So Why the Weirdness?

These words bend the rules because they're **culturally sacred** or **functionally critical**. "King," "Osiris," and "Beer" weren't just everyday nouns—they were woven into the **structure of Egyptian religion, politics, and daily life**.

When a word represents something that enormous, it gets treated differently. Hieroglyphs for these terms often carry special **stylistic, spiritual, or grammatical quirks**, like:
- Using determinatives in unexpected places
- Including silent or symbolic letters
- Prioritizing meaning over sound

It's like if we spelled "God" with a lightning bolt and a lion just to emphasize how powerful the idea is. Hieroglyphs didn't just record language—they **projected significance**.

Sometimes It's Not About the Rules

Language is always evolving—and so was hieroglyphic writing. Exceptions like *nswt*, *wsjr*, and *hnqt* show us that the scribes weren't just following a code—they were *expressing a worldview*.
So next time you spot an oddball glyph combo that doesn't quite add up, remember: it might just be one of Egypt's sacred exceptions, holding centuries of royal, divine, or fermented power.

One more to know: Baskets with Handles and it's two meanings
In the Egyptian writing system, most words follow consistent patterns—but just when you start to feel confident, you'll hit the **weird exceptions**. These are special cases where meaning can change entirely based on **position**, **context**, or **symbolic tradition**. Let's explore a particularly interesting

example: the word **"nb"** (𓎟), which can mean *lord…* or *thing.*

𓎟 The Basket without a Handle — "nb"

This symbol is called the **"basket without handle"** and it represents the sounds **n + b** — transliterated as **nb**. It's commonly translated as **"lord"**, **"master"**, or **"all"**, depending on where it shows up in a sentence.
The visual glyph looks like a woven basket with a curved handle:

𓎟 Gardiner Sign Code: V30
Sound: nb
Common Meanings: lord, all, every, master, thing

13. When 𓎟 Comes *Before* a Place Name

It typically means **"lord of"** that place.
Example:

𓎟𓂋𓏤 = *nb r* = "lord of the mouth"

𓎟𓂋𓈖𓏏𓊖 = *nb Rnt* = "lord of Renet"
More famously:

nb Abdws = *Lord of Abydos*

In this structure, the glyph **nb (𓎟)** functions almost like a title. It tells us the subject (often a king or god) holds dominion over the location that follows.

14. When 𓎟 Comes *After* a Word or Place

It can mean **"thing"** or **"all things."** It's abstract. It no longer acts as a title but becomes a noun.
Example:

𓏏𓊖𓎟 = *t3 nb*
= "every thing (of the land)" or "all things of the land"
Another:

𓅓𓂋𓎟 = *m r nb* = "in every mouth" (a poetic phrase meaning something like "on everyone's lips")

Let's Break That Down

Glyph Transliteration Meaning

Nb   lord / all / thing

t³   land or place

t³ nb   "all things of the land"

Position matters. Put ⌣ first, it's about **power**. Put it after, it's about **totality**

Why Does This Matter?

Understanding exceptions like **nb (⌣)** helps decode real inscriptions—on tombs, temples, or museum pieces. Egyptian isn't just a language—it's **symbolic art**. Meaning can flip with a glyph's position, especially when a word wears multiple hats (like "lord" and "thing").
It's a little like how English uses "light" for both "illumination" and "not heavy." Context is everything!

Chapter 22: Modern Uses and Fun Projects

Bringing Hieroglyphs into Your Life (Without Needing a Pyramid)

Hieroglyphs didn't vanish with the pharaohs—they just went underground for a few thousand years. Now, with pop culture, digital art, and the internet, they're back, and they're more versatile than ever. From museums to memes, from tattoos to TikTok, people are using hieroglyphs not only to honor the past but to make the present more meaningful. This chapter is your invitation to join that movement—and to create projects that feel authentic, fun, and totally you.

Where Hieroglyphs Show Up Today
    Video Games
- *Assassin's Creed Origins* and *Sphinx and the Cursed Mummy* use real hieroglyphs for clues, quests, and immersion.
- Gamers are decoding glyphs on temples and treasure chests—sometimes they're real Egyptian phrases!
    Movies and TV
- In *Moon Knight*, *The Mummy*, and *Stargate*, hieroglyphs are more than set dressing—they're used in puzzles, magic spells, and portals.
- The glyphs add authenticity and *mystery*—and you now know how to read some of them!
    Social Media
- Artists and educators share glyph-doodles, quotes, affirmations, and TikToks about how to read hieroglyphs.
- You can find your name in hieroglyphs in Instagram filters or print it on T-shirts.

You're no longer a tourist to this world. You're a citizen of it.

How You Can Use Hieroglyphs
    In Your Journal or Sketchbook
- Start each journal entry with the date in glyphs.
- Use glyphs to track moods, dreams, or spiritual goals.
- Add "protection glyphs" to pages about fears or challenges (like scarabs, ankhs, or hands).
    In Your Art
- Incorporate glyphs into your digital art, collage, zines, or murals.
- Design a character whose powers come from glyphs (basically *Yu-Gi-Oh* with ancient flair).
- Make hieroglyphic comic strips or visual poems.
    In Decor or Fashion
- Print or paint glyphs on your walls, notebooks, or shoes.
- Design glyph tattoos (temporary or real!) that represent values or affirmations.
- Create your own "amulet" or charm with symbols for strength, growth, or peace.

Glyph Projects to Try
    15. Hieroglyphic Affirmation Poster
- Choose 3 values: e.g., courage, truth, transformation.
- Find glyphs that represent them (lion, feather, scarab).
- Arrange them in balance, add color, and frame it as your daily reminder.
    16. Glyph-Based Tarot or Oracle Cards

- Assign a glyph to a concept (Ankh = Life, Snake = Change, Sun = Clarity).
- Create a mini deck and draw a card for guidance.
- Journal about how that glyph applies to your day.

17. Name Banner in Cartouches
- Write your name and those of your friends or pets in cartouches.
- Add titles like "Guardian of Snacks" or "Queen of Vibes."
- Hang them in your room or give them as fun gifts.

18. Digital Sticker Pack
- Create hieroglyph stickers using a drawing app.
- Include emojis, uniliterals, cartouches, and offering hands.
- Upload them for use in messages or on social media.

Gift Idea: Make a personalized glyph scroll for someone's birthday or graduation!

Make It Your Own

Don't feel limited to historical accuracy. The ancient Egyptians didn't just copy—they innovated. They invented new glyphs, added flair, and evolved over centuries. You can too.
- Want to invent a glyph for "Wi-Fi" or "coffee"? Go for it.
- Want to remix classic glyphs into your art style? Do it.
- Want to write a short story or comic in glyphs? You have all the tools now.
-

Doodler's Manifesto:

Hieroglyphs are yours now. Not as museum pieces, but as tools of expression, imagination, and personal storytelling.

Challenge: The Doodling With Purpose Project

Create a final piece that combines everything:
1. Your name in a cartouche
2. A short phrase in hieroglyphs (blessing, quote, or affirmation)
3. At least 3 symbolic glyphs with sacred meaning
4. Balanced layout like a stela or temple wall
5. Optional: date it using Egyptian calendar format

Use it as:
- A page in your journal
- A scroll for your wall
- A social media post
- A message to your future self

Then… share it. Or keep it private. Either way, you've done something amazing.

Part 3: DOODLING 101: How to Draw Hieroglyphics

How to Draw the Owl Glyph (𓅓) – The Letter "M"

Hieroglyph: 𓅓
Sound: "m"
Glyph   **Name:**   Owl
Meaning: The consonant "M" – very common in names and words.

Materials:

- Pencil or pen
- Paper or sketchbook
- Optional: eraser, fine liner for final detailing

Step-by-Step Guide:

Step 1: Draw the Head

- Begin with a **rounded square or dome shape** for the owl's head.
- Leave the **bottom open** to connect with the body later.
- Add two **large circular eyes** toward the top of the head.
- Sketch a small **triangle-shaped beak** pointing downward between the eyes.

Step 2: Draw the Body

- From the head, draw a **rounded rectangle or oval shape** for the body.
- Make the owl **squat and compact**, not tall or narrow.
- Leave a **small gap at the bottom** to add feet later.

Step 3: Add Wing Details

- Draw two curved lines from either side of the owl's body, sloping gently downward.
- These are the folded **wings**.
- Inside the wing shapes, sketch **simple feather lines** (3-4 vertical or curved strokes).

Step 4: Draw the Feet

- Draw two **short legs** sticking out beneath the body.
- Add **3 toes** on each foot, slightly curved—like the letter "w" facing down.

Step 5: Add Facial Features

- Darken the **pupils** inside the eyes.

- Optionally, shade around the eyes for contrast.
- Add tiny feathery lines on the chest and around the beak to suggest fluff.

Step 6: Finalize and Ink (Optional)

- Trace over your drawing with a pen or fine liner.
- Erase pencil lines for a clean finish.
- Shade or decorate based on real Egyptian carvings—or add your own style!

Visual Tips:

- Keep the owl's **body symmetrical**.
- Egyptian owls often have a slightly **stern or wide-eyed look**—don't make it too cartoonish unless that's your style.
- You can stylize the feet and wings, but **always emphasize the broad shape and face**.

Bonus Idea:

Use the owl glyph in your name if it contains the letter **M**—then practice drawing the **cartouche** around it to give it a royal to

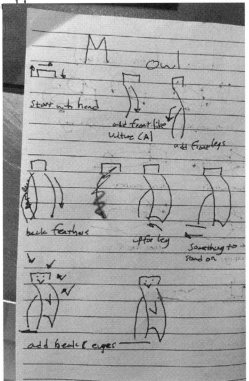

How to Draw Like a Scribe (Without Going to Scribe School)

So, you've drawn an owl. 🦉 You've entered the glyph-iverse. Welcome to the next level: the *How-To-Doodle Deep Dive*. This is where we move beyond just reading hieroglyphs and actually start **drawing them like the ancient pros**.

First, Let's Talk Order

You might think drawing hieroglyphs is just copying cool pictures. Start with the eyes, maybe add a beak, scribble in some feathers, done! Right?

Nope. Turns out, **there's a system**.

Egyptologists—true glyph nerds—have analyzed **chisel marks, brush strokes, and paint layers** on temple walls and papyrus to figure out how each glyph was created. And just like cursive letters or kung fu moves, **glyphs have a proper stroke order**. You don't freestyle a scarab beetle. You build it from the shell out.

Why? Because ancient scribes were trained for *years* to ensure glyphs looked precise, balanced, and proportional—even on the side of a cliff. Think of it like building LEGO sets. You *can* start with the head, but you're going to regret it when the legs won't snap on.

What We're About to Do

This section is your **drawing dojo**. We're about to look at **hand-drawn versions of every major uniliteral glyph**, plus a curated selection of **biliterals**, **triliterals**, and even some crowd-favorite determinatives like the ankh ☥ and the ever-iconic scarab 🪲 (don't worry, you'll get there).

Out of the *200+ sound glyphs* in the Egyptian writing system, I've chosen **the most fun, most tricky, or most versatile ones** to focus on. Some are templates—once you know how to draw one **herb**, you can draw ten. Once you master one **animal body**, the rest follow like Pokémon evolutions.

Spoiler: **always start animal glyphs at the base of the neck**. Trust me. You'll thank me when you're five legs in and things are still symmetrical.

A Word About My Handwriting

Real talk? My handwriting is terrible. If hieroglyphs were judged by an art professor, I'd be kicked out of the tomb. But this book isn't about being perfect—**it's about learning by doodling**.

So what you'll see next are:
- **Scans from my actual hieroglyph sketch diary**
- **Step-by-step breakdowns** of how to draw select glyphs
- **Pro tips** scribbled in the margins (because real learning is messy)

Not *every* glyph will have a detailed step-by-step (I'm not a robot), but if you can master **these 100 or so**, you'll have a working visual language that opens up the rest.

TL;DR – Doodle Like a Demigod

- There's a **correct order** to drawing glyphs (start at the right place, end with flair).
- We know this from **archaeology and brushstroke analysis**.
- What follows is a hand-drawn crash course through the glyph galaxy.
- You don't need to be an artist. You just need to be curious.
- **Practice. Laugh. Repeat.**

Now grab your pen, stylus, or chisel (if you're hardcore), and let's make some sacred scribbles. Or, you know, just keep drawing owls. That works too.

'a or 3 = f<u>a</u>ther   s = ro<u>s</u>e or <u>z</u>oo

⁶a or ⁶ = p<u>a</u>lm   ś = <u>s</u>oap

    b = <u>b</u>ook   š = <u>s</u>how

    d = <u>d</u>og

    d̲ = j as in le<u>dg</u>e   t = <u>t</u>urtle

    f = <u>f</u>rank   t̲ = <u>tj</u> or <u>z</u> like la<u>tch</u>

    g = <u>g</u>oat

    h = <u>h</u>ome   w = <u>w</u>ater or r<u>u</u>le

    h· = <u>h</u>iss'd (hss)   y = <u>y</u>es or c<u>i</u>ty

    h̲ = ch as in Ba<u>ch</u> (kh)

    h̲ = ch as in <u>h</u>ue

i or í = <u>y</u>es or mach<u>i</u>ne

    k = <u>k</u>ing

    k· = <u>Qu</u>een

    l = <u>l</u>ion

  m = <u>m</u>om

  n = <u>n</u>o

  p = <u>P</u>op

  r = <u>r</u>am

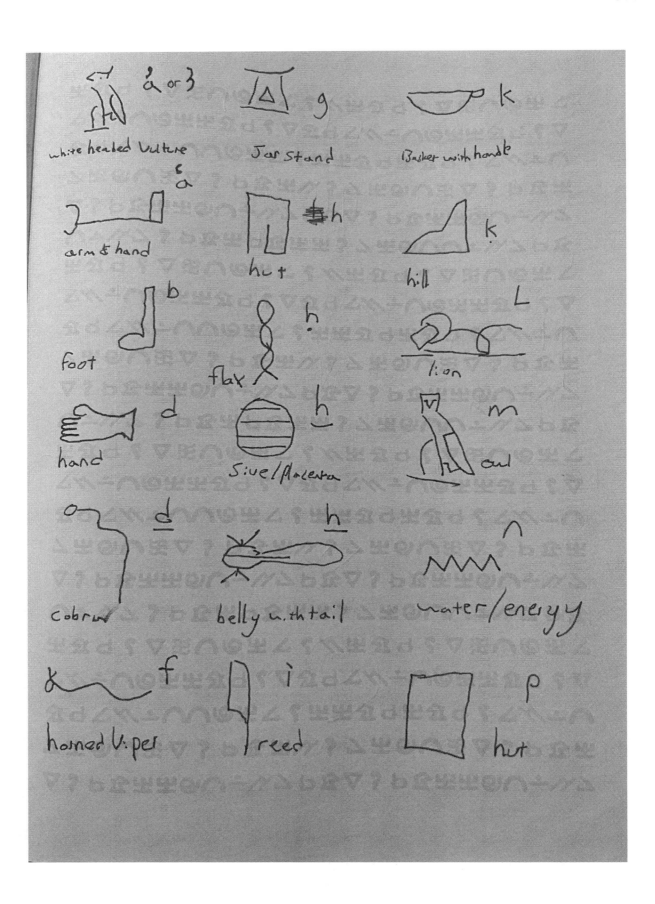

ȝ or 3 — white headed vulture

g — Jar Stand

k — Basket with handle

ꜥ — arm & hand

h — hut

ḳ — hill

b — foot

ḥ — flax

L — lion

d — hand

ḫ — Sive/Placenta

m — owl

ḏ — cobra

ẖ — belly with tail

water/energy

f — horned viper

i — reed

p — hut

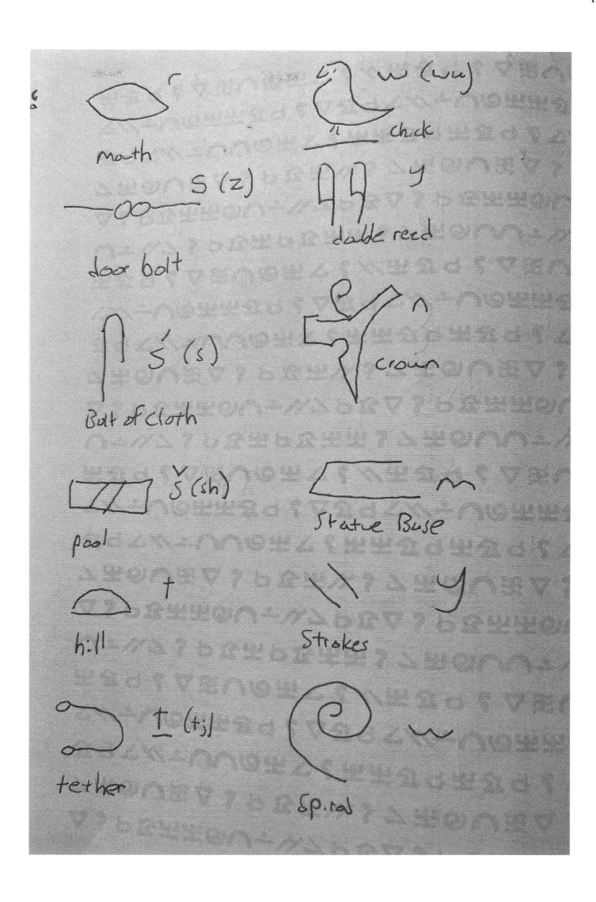

mouth ꜥ

w (wu)
chick

S (z)
door bolt

y
double reed

Ś (s)
Bolt of cloth

crown

Š (sh)
pool

Statue Base

t
hill

Strokes

Ṯ (tj)
tether

Spiral

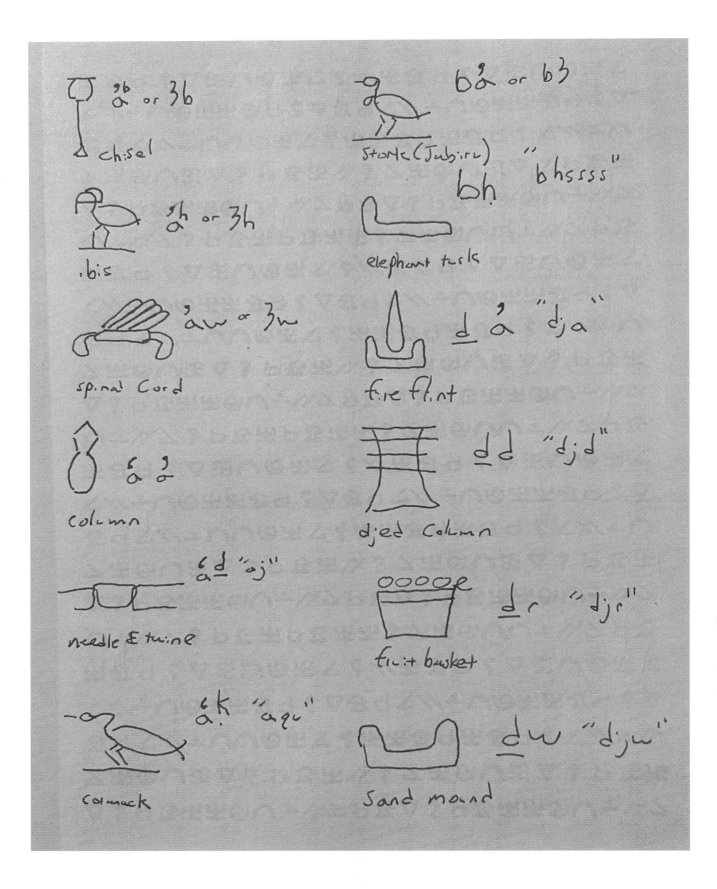

116

ꜣb or 3b — chisel

bꜣ or b3 — stone (Jabiru)

ꜣḫ or 3ḫ — ibis

bḥ "bhsss" — elephant tusk

ꜥw or 3w — spinal cord

ḏꜣ "dja" — fire flint

ꜥꜣ — column

ḏd "djd" — djed column

ꜥḏ "ŏj" — needle & twine

ḏr "djr" — fruit basket

ꜥq "aqu" — cormack

ḏw "dju" — sand mound

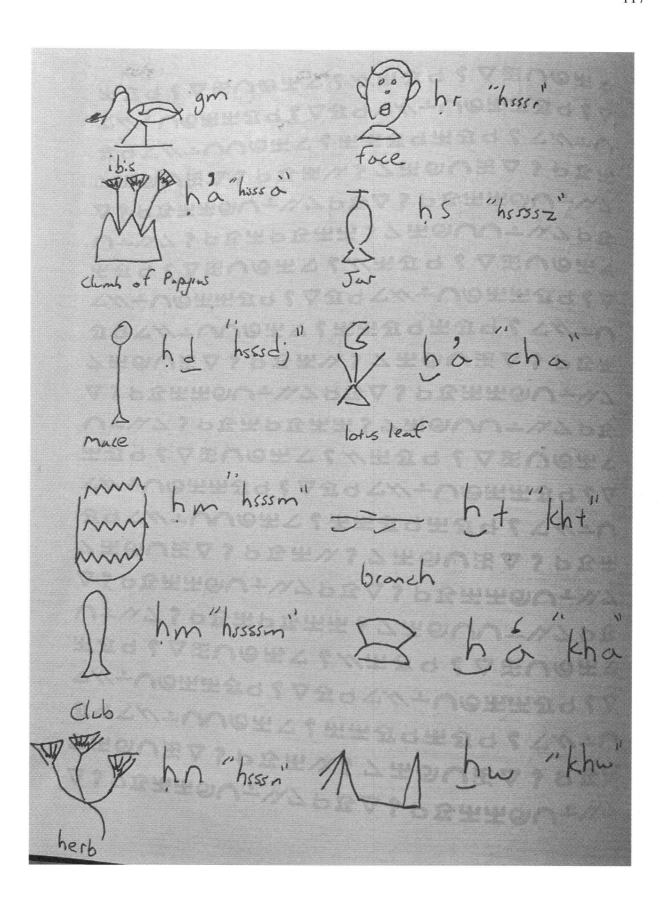

gm

ibis

ḥr "hsssr"

face

ḥˤȝ "hsssˤ"

Clumps of Papyrus

ḥs "hsrssz"

Jar

ḥḏ "hsssdj"

Mace

ḥˤ "cha"

lotus leaf

ḥm "hsssm"

ḫt "kht"

branch

ḥm "hsssm"

Club

ḥˤ "kha"

ḥn "hssn"

herb

ḫw "khw"

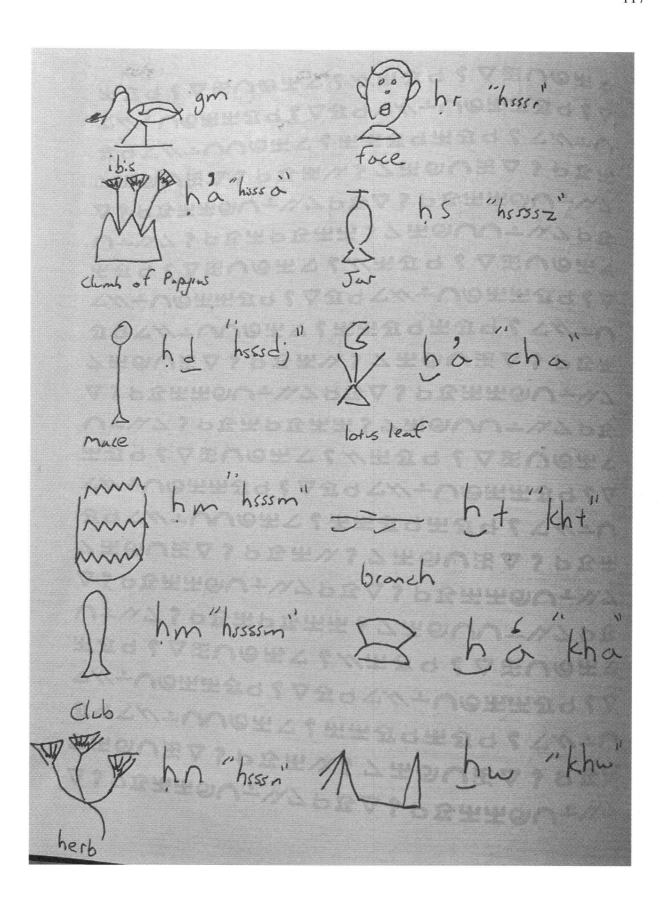

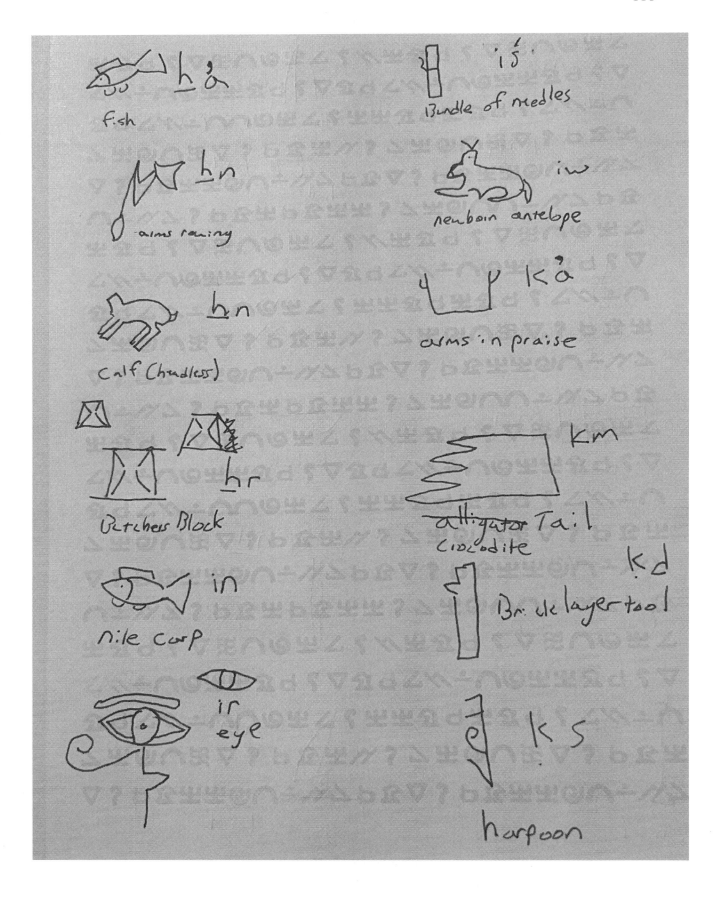

fish — ḥ à

arms rowing — ḥn

calf (headless) — ḥn

Butchers Block — ḥr

nile carp — in

ir
eye

Bundle of needles — is

newborn antelope — iw

arms in praise — kà

alligator Tail — km
crocodile

Bride layer tool — kd

harpoon — ks

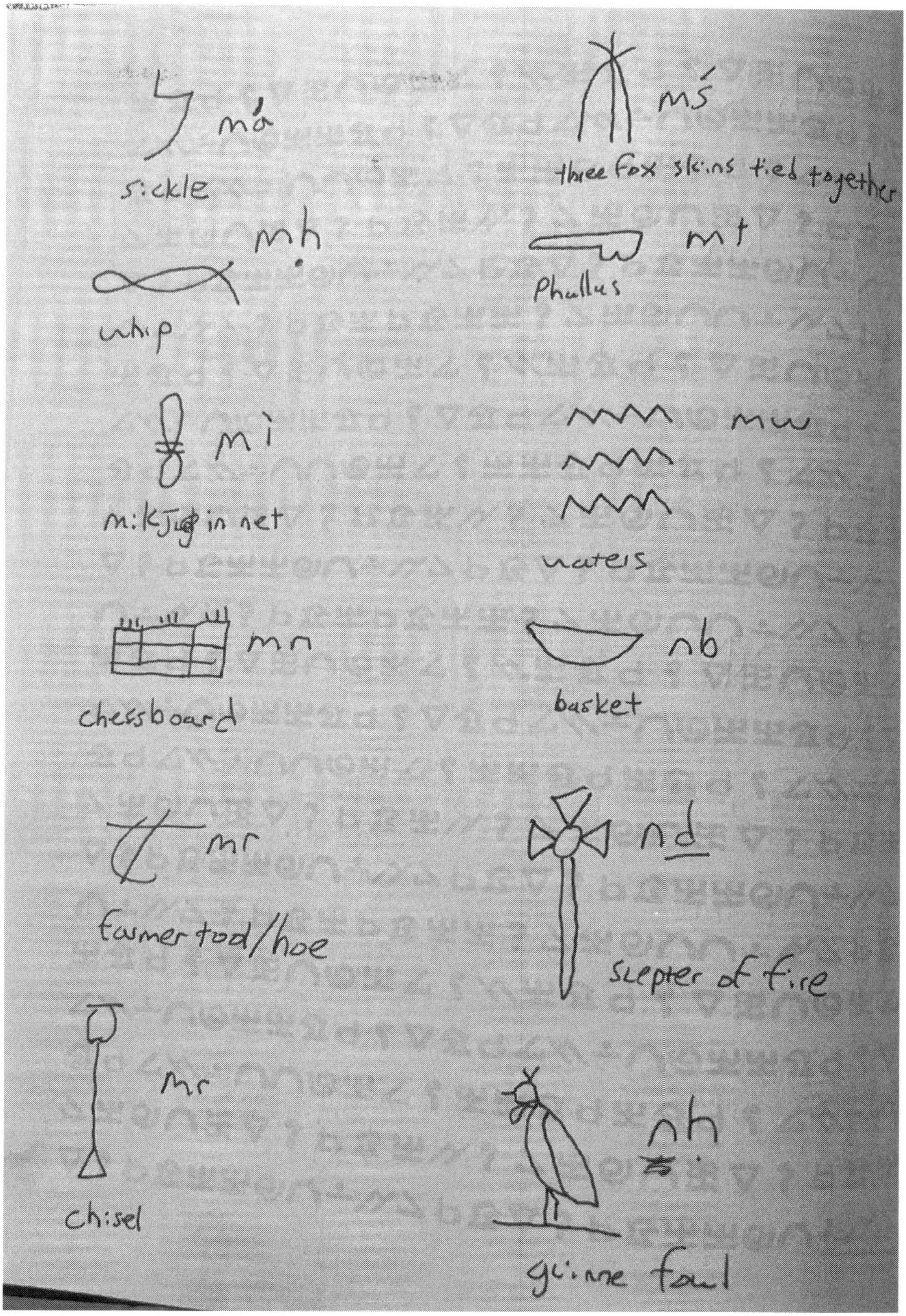

mꜣ
sickle

mḥ
whip

mi
mikju in net

mn
chessboard

mr
farmer tod/hoe

mr
chisel

mś
three fox skins tied together

mt
Phallus

mw
waters

nb
basket

nḏ
scepter of fire

nḥ
guinne fowl

nm
butcher knife

nn
rush shoots

nś
ox tongue

nw/in
bowl

Pꜣ
pin tail duck in flight

Ph
hindquarters of lion

house plan
Pr

rw
recumbant lion

Sꜣ
pintail duck

Sꜣ
looped cord to hold cattle

Sꜣ
lid

Śk
Broom

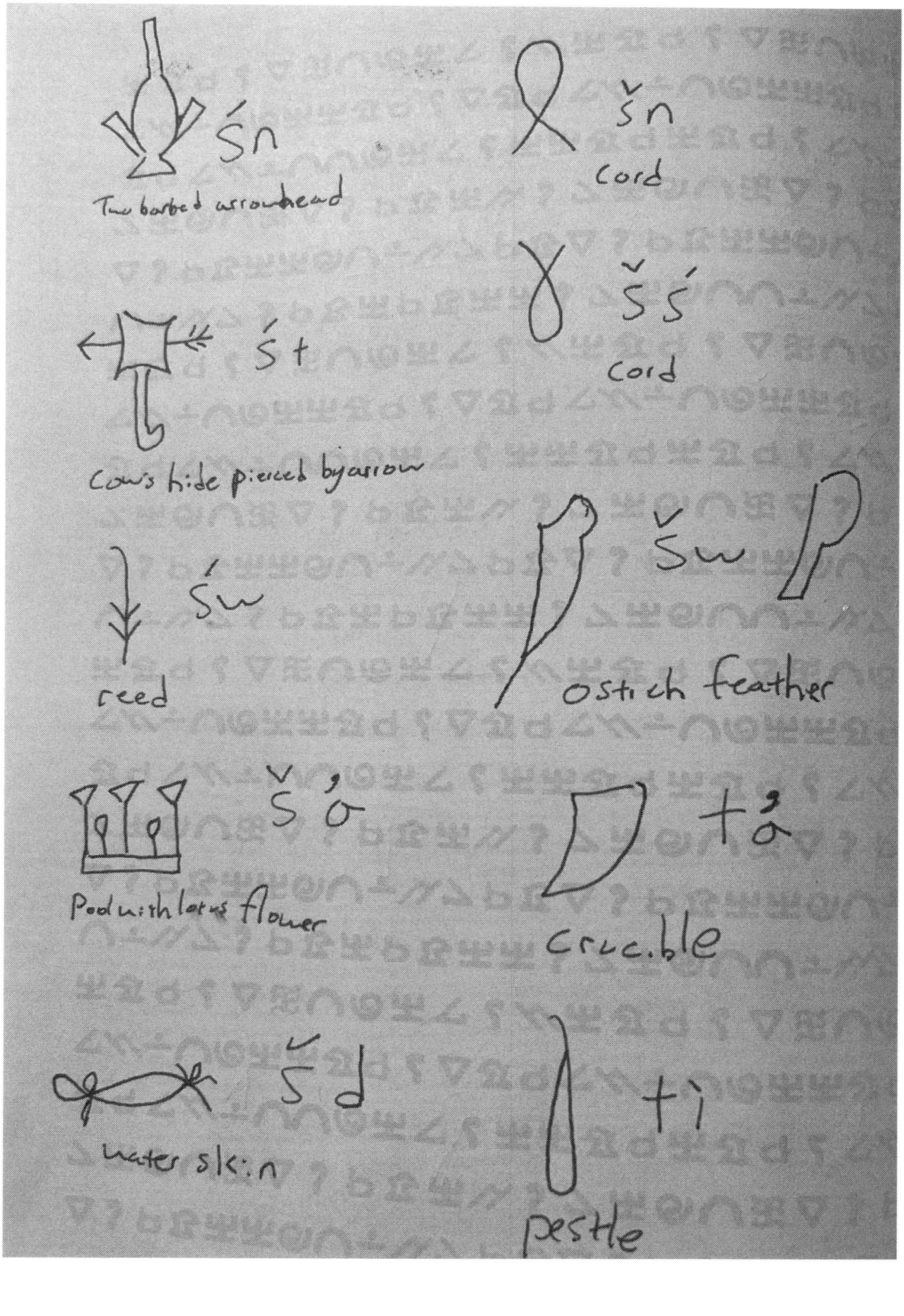

śn

Two barbed arrowhead

š̌n

cord

śt

Cow's hide pierced by arrow

š̌ś

cord

św

reed

š̌w

ostrich feather

š̌ʿ

Pod with lotus flower

tʿ

crucible

śd

water skin

ti

pestle

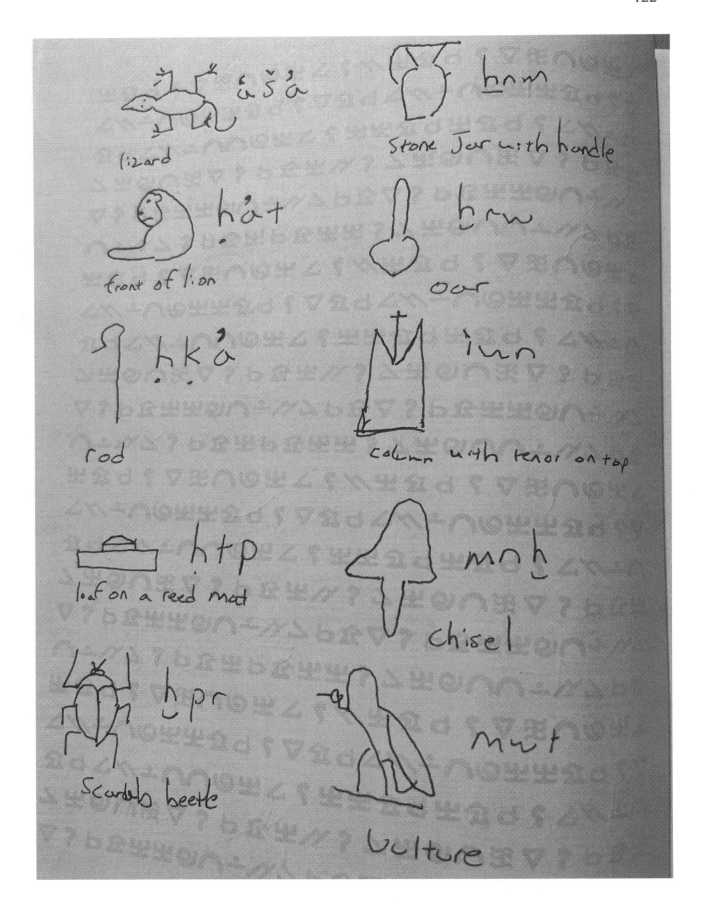

ꜥšꜣ

lizard

ẖnm

Stone Jar with handle

ḥꜣt

front of lion

ḫrw

oar

ḥkꜣ

rod

iwn

column with tenor on top

ḥtp

loaf on a reed mat

mnḫ

chisel

ḫpr

Scarab beetle

mwt

vulture

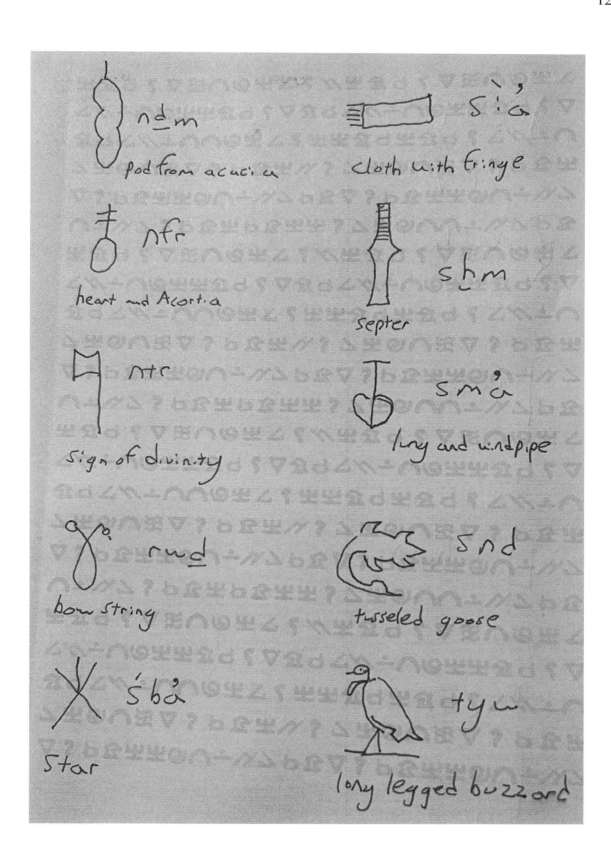

ndm
pod from acacia

s'a
cloth with fringe

nfr
heart and Aortia

shm
septer

ntr
sign of divinity

sma
lung and windpipe

rud
bow string

snd
tasseled goose

s'ba
star

tyw
long legged buzzard

wꜣḏ

stem of papyrus

wꜥḥ

Broom

wꜣś

scepter

wḥm

leg of ox

wśr

scepter

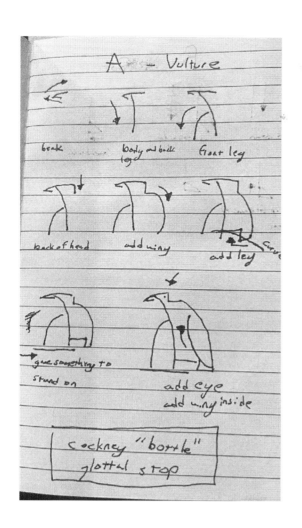

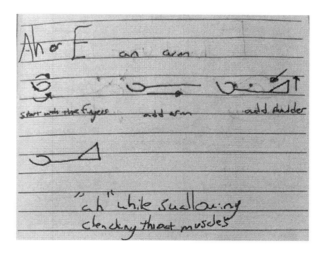

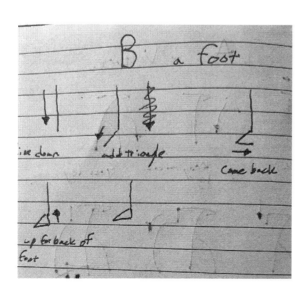

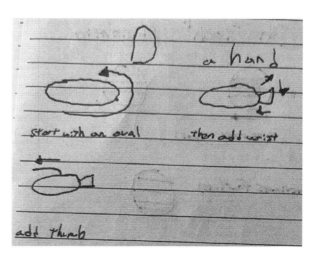

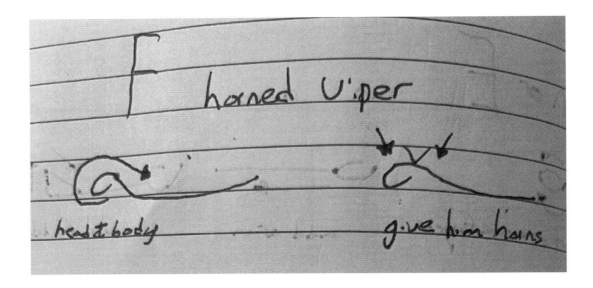

F — horned Viper

head & body   give him horns

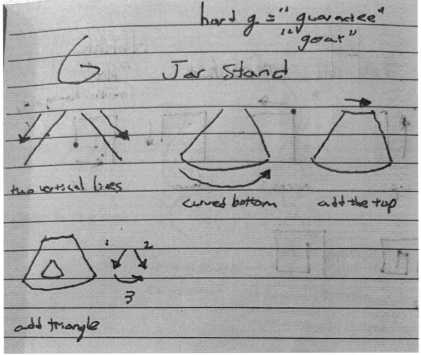

hard g = "guarantee"
"goat"

G — Jar Stand

two vertical lines   curved bottom   add the top

add triangle

This Glyph represents an ancient Egyptian jar stand. When you see one in a museum you will recognize it right away! A good example of "the Egyptian Mind" that created these.

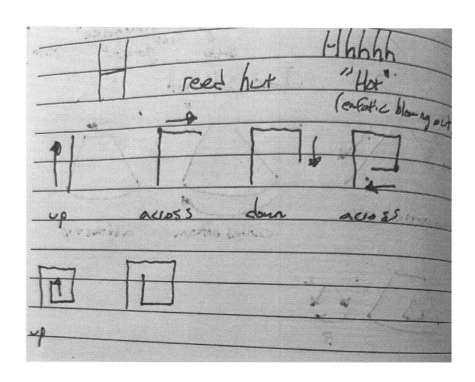

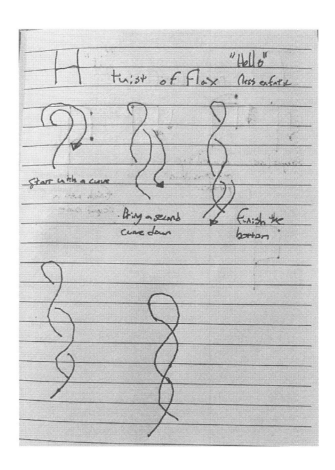

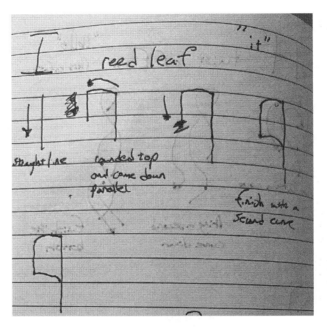

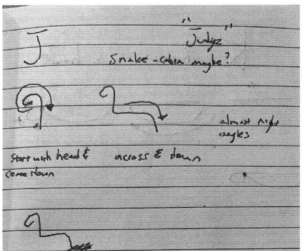

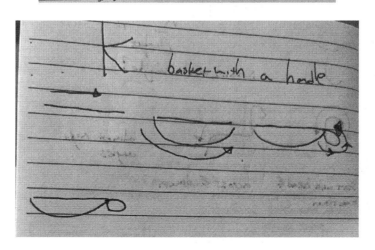

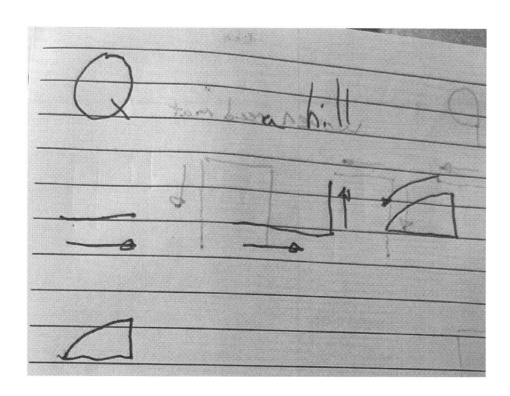

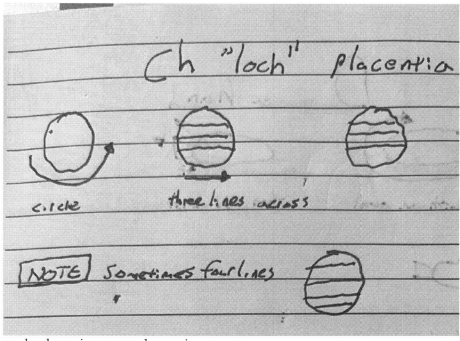

This Glyph has also been interpreted as a sieve.

The "L" glyph below was created late in the new kingdom to accommodate Alexander the Great's name. There are no L words or names in ancient Egyptian!

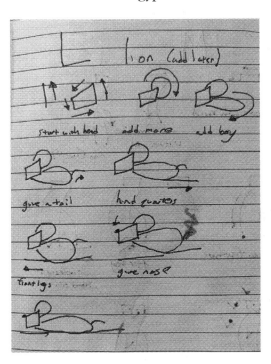

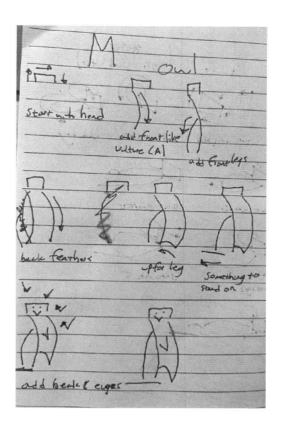

M   Owl

Start with head

add front like vulture (A)

add front legs

back feathers

up for leg

Something to stand on

add beak & eyes

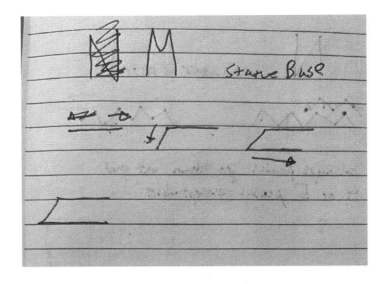

The statue base is a common alternative for M.
The Owl is much more common.

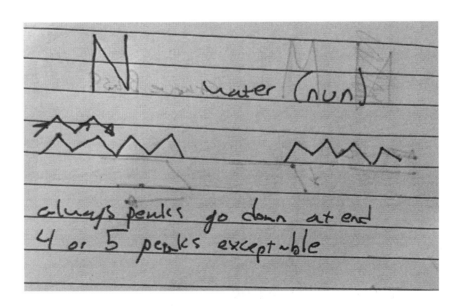

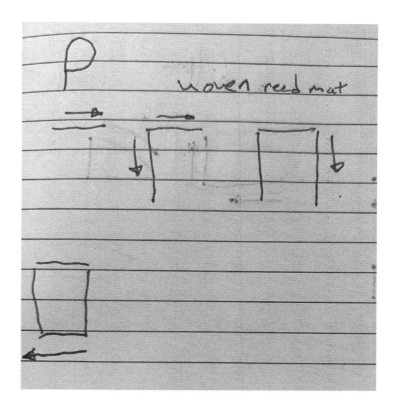

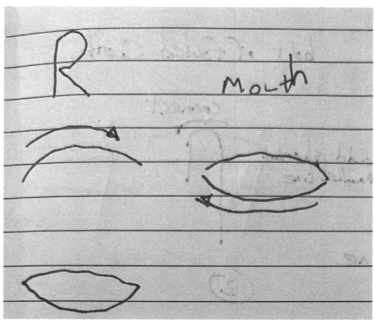

The Mouth glyph can also be used for a person's job or station, as in "the person who speaks and gives the rules/directions".

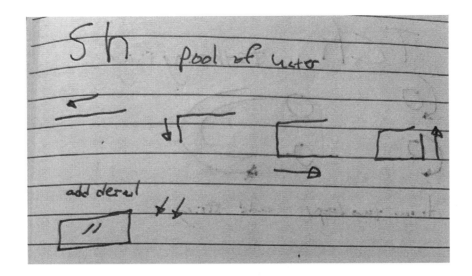

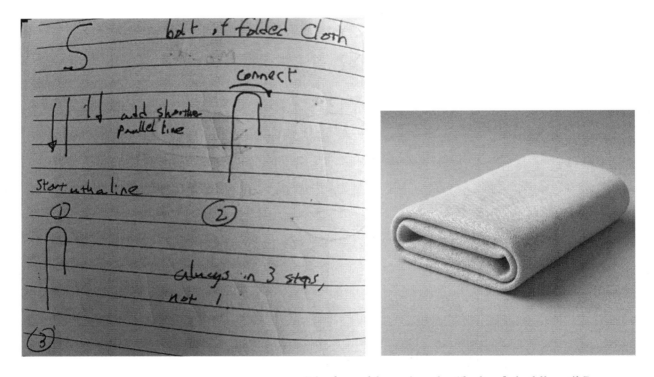

I had trouble seeing the "bolt of cloth" until I saw one.

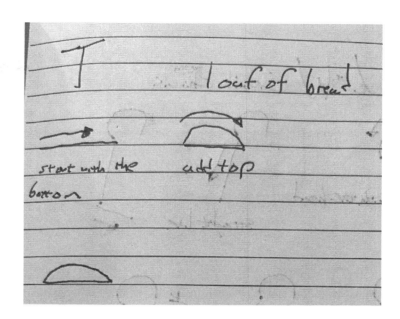

The loaf glyph is used at the end of names to indicate a female. It is silent in this form.

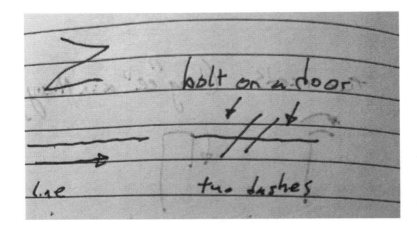

The quail chick below is often used to pluralize words like the English "s".

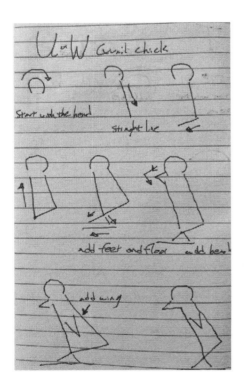

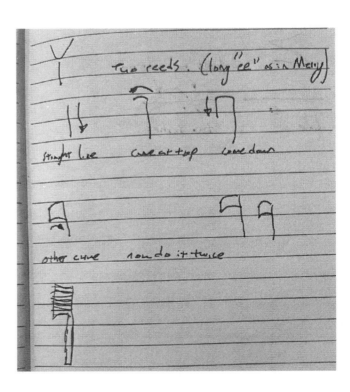

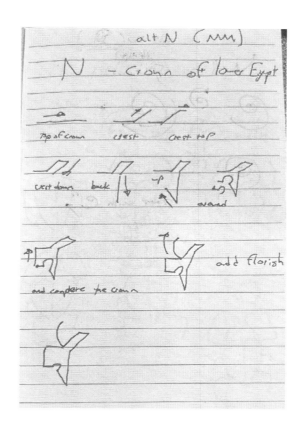

alt N (ᴎᴎᴎ)

N - Crown of lower Egypt

top of crown   crest   crest top

crest down   back   onward

and complete the crown   add florish

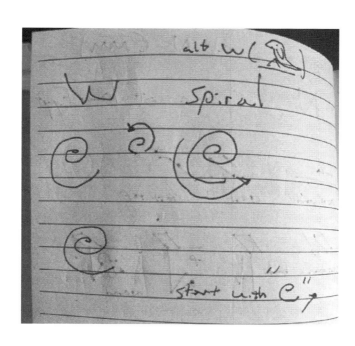

alt w (🐦)

W   spiral

start with "C"

Select Bilateral and Trilateral Signs

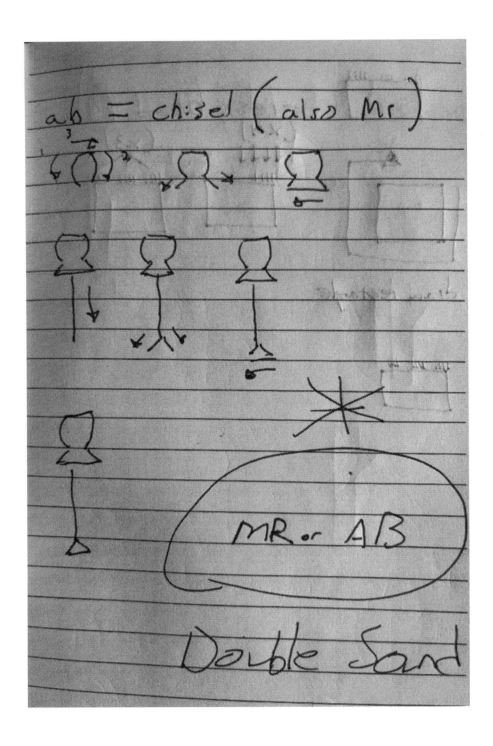

ah - ibis crested

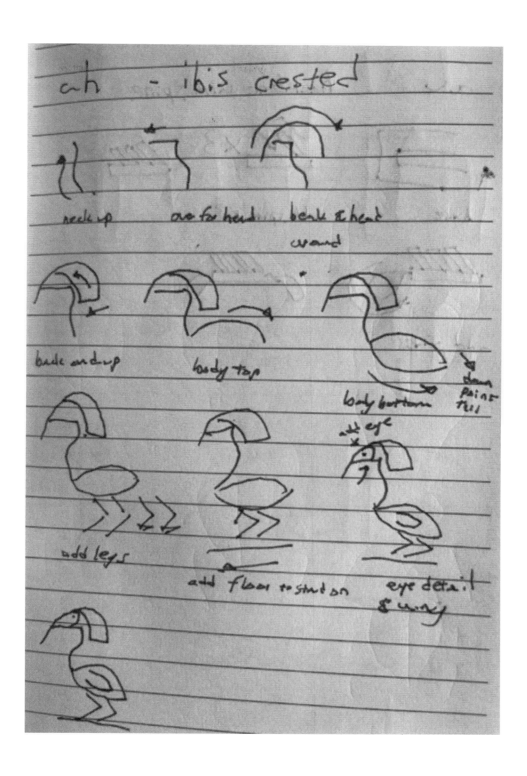

neck up   axe for head   beak & head
                                            crowned

back and up   body top   body bottom   them
                                                                                 paint
                                                                                 tail

                                            add eye
add legs   eye detail
                        add floor to stand on   & wing

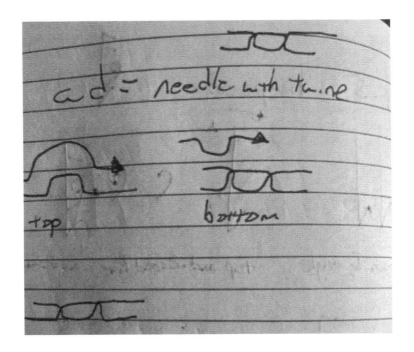

a d = needle with twine

top

bottom

ak cormamet

leg de

add tail

bird Stork

Straight leg

angle leg

other foot

something to stand on

insert wing like a Z

gullet

head

beak

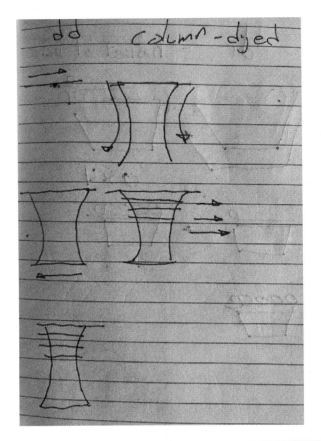

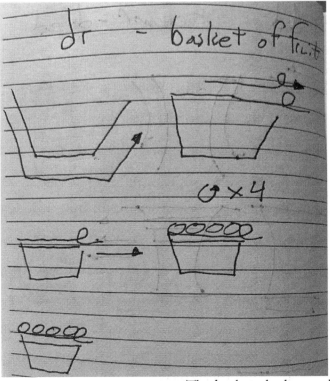

The basket glyph can also be the word "since".

hn — herb

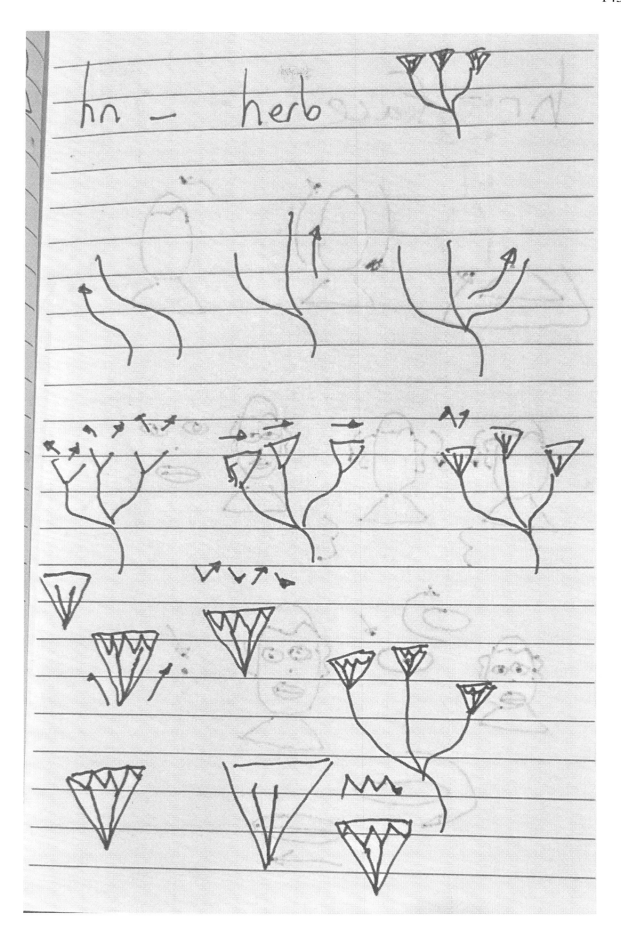

144

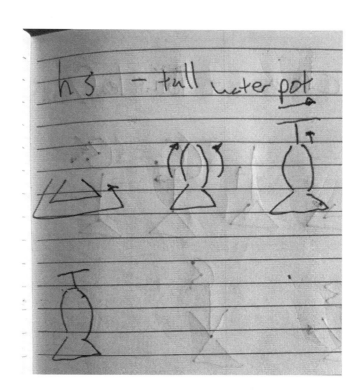

The glyph below also us used for the number 1,000.

cht + branch

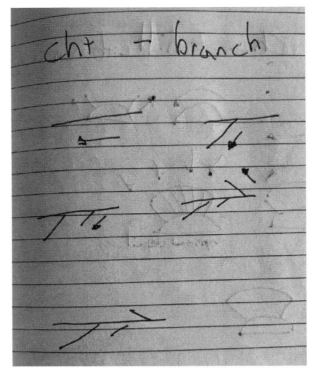

hur. arm with whip/flagellum
Flagellum

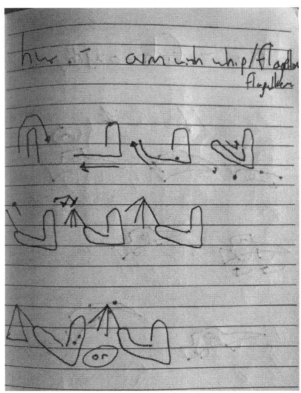

or

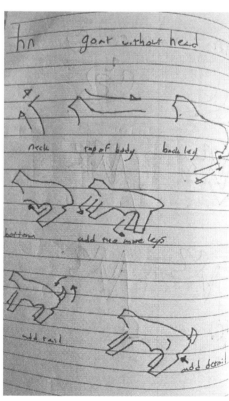

hn —butcher's Blocks

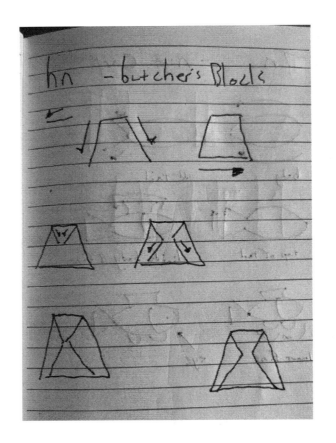

In —nile Carp

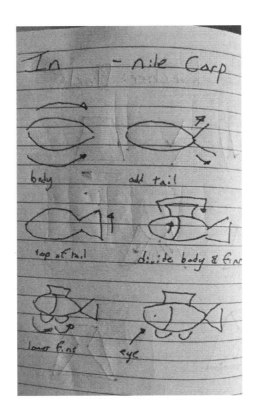

body   add tail

top of tail   divide body & fins

lower fins   eye

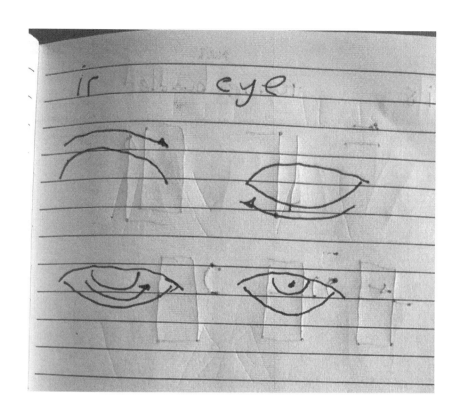

eye

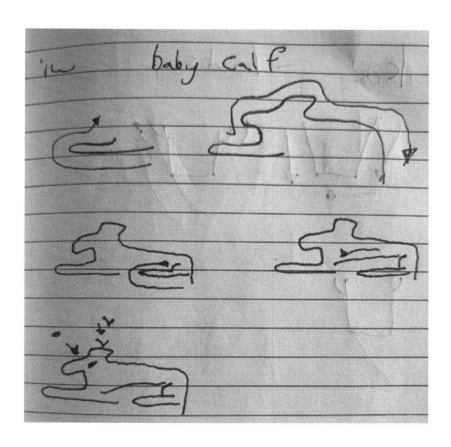

baby calf

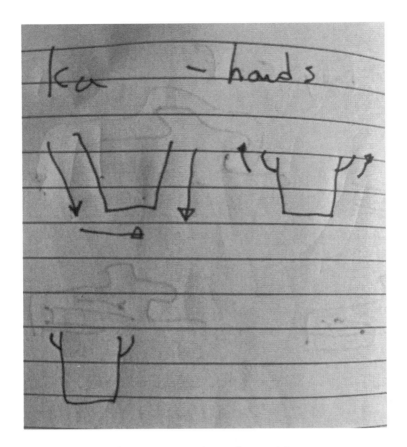

A "Ka" is one's soul or spirit.

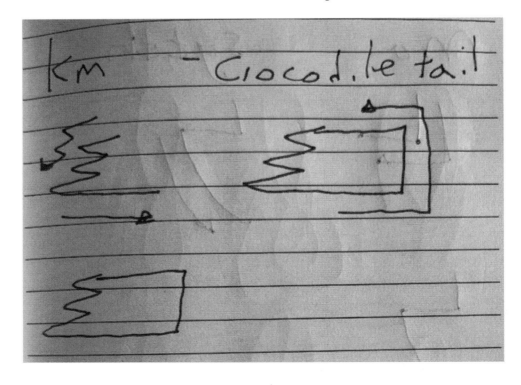

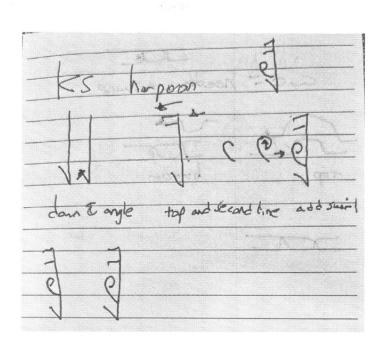

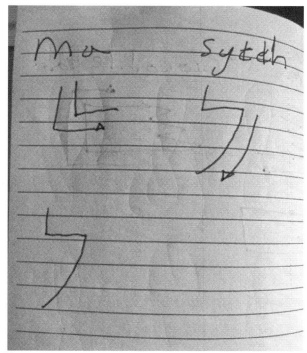

You will see this glyph at the start of the word "to see" (maaa).

MR is used for the word love and is one of the more common double sounds.

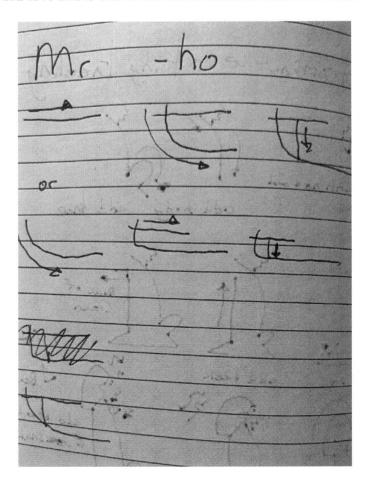

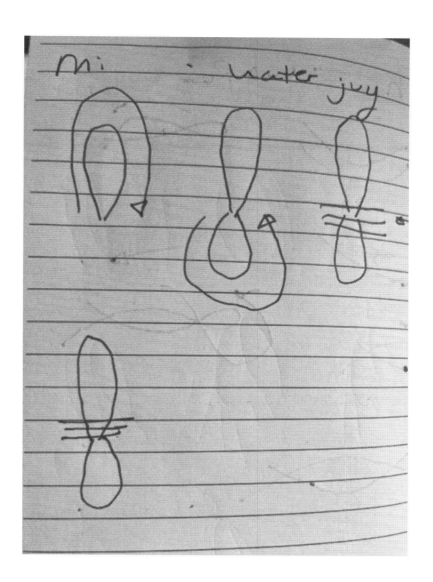

mi water juy

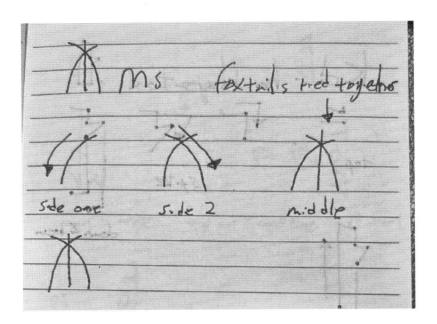

ms   foxtails tree together

side one   side 2   middle

nd - staff

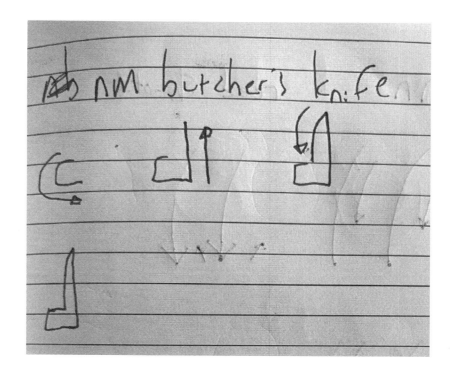

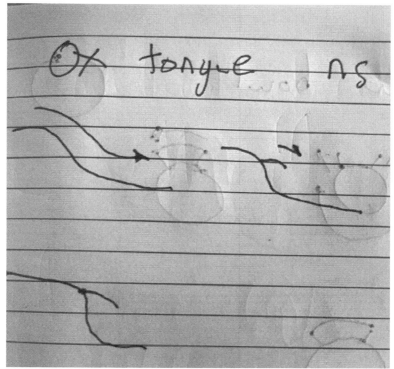

The Ox tongue can also be used in place of the mouth glyph for R as the tongue is in the mouth and does the speaking.

nw basket

Pa   pintail duck flying

PR is one of the most common Glyphs and is used for both sound and an ideogram.

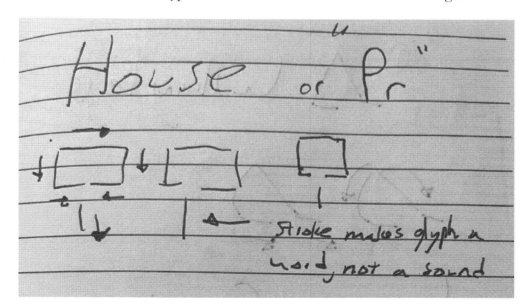

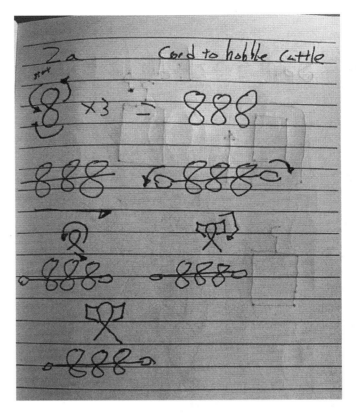

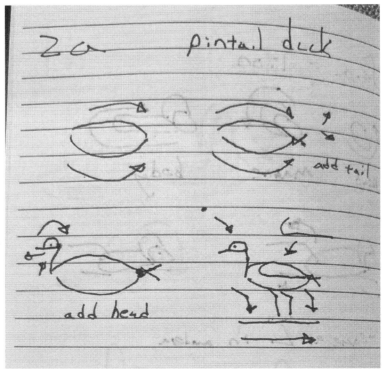

Often used for the word son or add a T (loaf) for daughter.

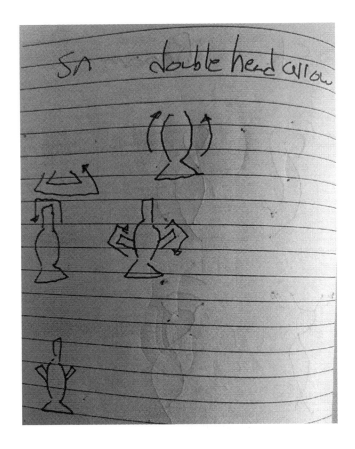

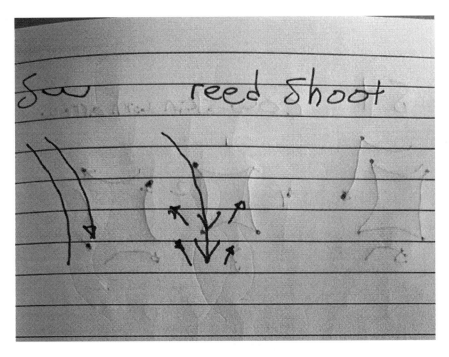

This glyph is used to start off the common spelling of "king". Important one to know!

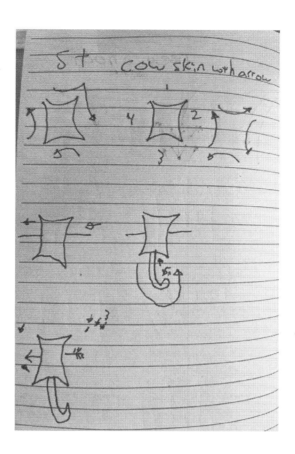

The lasso glyph below is often used by amateur readers as the single sound "o", but it is more of an "WAughooo" sound.

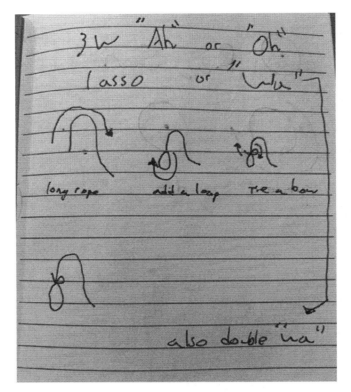

This feather glyph is used on a lot of stella and reliefs as the weight in which a man must weigh his life's sins against in the afterlife. Note the difference between this and the reed used for (i) and (y).

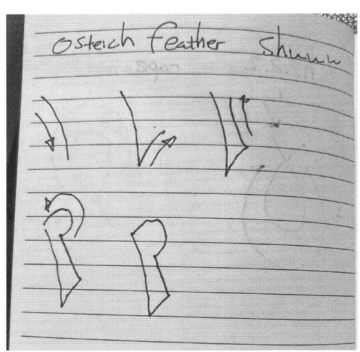

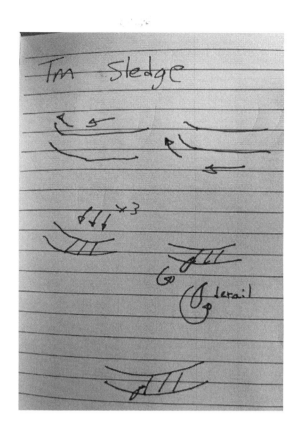

Sometimes it helps to make up little memory tools. For the sledge I think of it as "Tim's Sled" or Tim owns a sled to recall the sound of "tm".

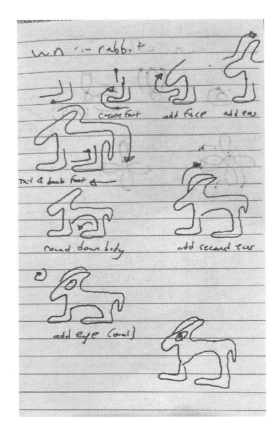

I will be the first to confess that my rabbit is not very good. I have gotten much better, the body I too thin in this drawing! All animals with four legs (and most a determinatives) one should always start at the nap of the neck and go up to the head and around to the back.

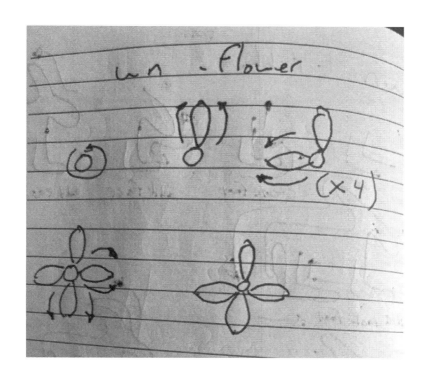

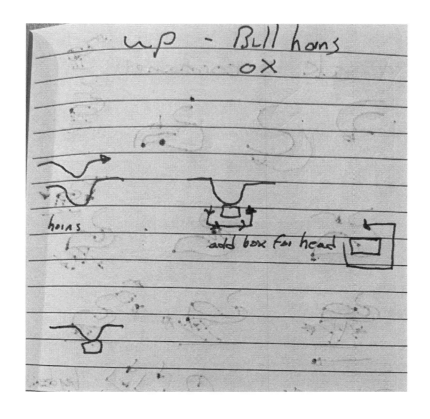

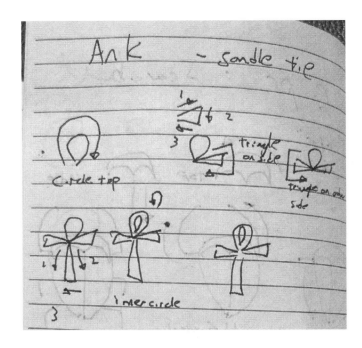

Here they are, two of the most famous glyphs of all, the Ankh and the Scarab Beetle.

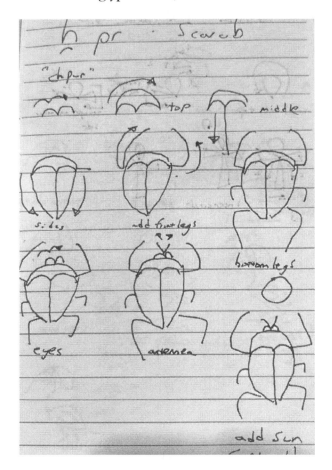

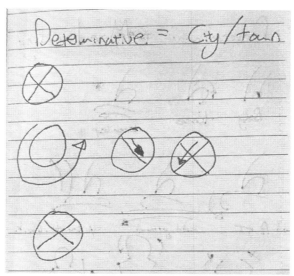

This is one of my favorite determinatives. Remember when Indy said "X never marks the spot."? Well this is where it started! All towns and places are noted with a circle and an X through it. This is where we get the origin of every treasure map ever!

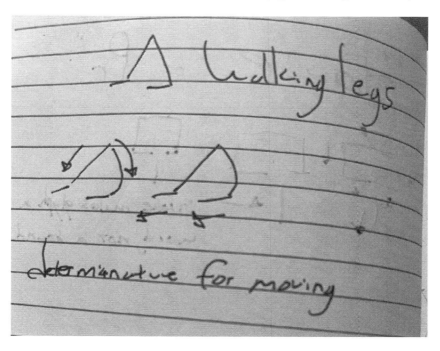

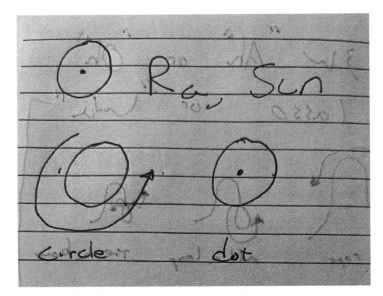

Ra Sun

circle   dot

Determinative = Man kneeling

body   knee   low leg

add Butt   add ground   up for the back

add neck   add head   add arms

face detail   add eye

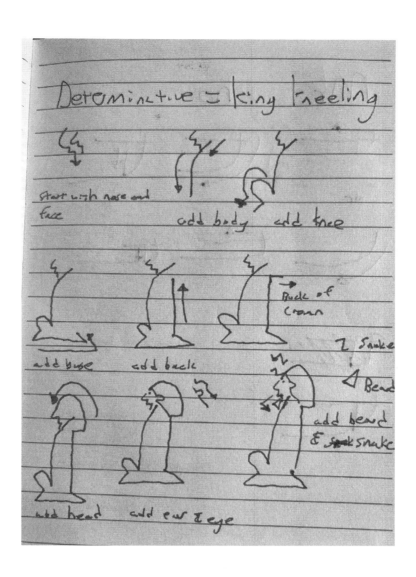

Determinative ⚵ King kneeling

Start with nose and face

add body   add knee

add base   add back

Back of Crown

⎔ Snake

△ Beard

add head   add ear & eye

add beard & snake

Part 4: Appendixes

Appendix A: Complete Uniliteral Sign List

The Egyptian Alphabet – One Sound, One Symbol

Sound Hieroglyph		Glyph Description	Transliteration Notes
	Vulture	Glottal stop (')	Often appears at the start of names
	Reed leaf	"i" or "y" sound	Functions like both vowel and consonant
	Forearm	"a" (as in "father")	Often silent but still present
	Foot	"b"	Straightforward consonant
	Twisted flax	"h"	Light h sound
	Placenta	"kh" or "x" sound	Like German "Bach"
	Horned viper	"f"	Sharp f-sound
	Owl	"m"	Common in names
	Water ripple	"n"	Often seen in plural and location words
	Stool	"p"	Associated with "per" (house)
	Mouth	"r"	Rolled r (often interchangeable with l)
	Folded cloth	"s"	Common consonant
	Pool or lake	"sh"	Sh-sound as in "ship"
	Bread loaf	"t"	Feminine word marker
	Tethering rope	"ṭ" or emphatic t	Emphasized sound, rare
	Hand	"d"	Appears often in "give" (di)
	Cobra	"dj" or "g" (like "j" in "jam")	Can be softened to "ch" or "j"
	Basket with handle	"k"	Hard k-sound
	Jar Stand	"g" (hard g, as in "go")	Rare, used mostly in names

	r bolt	"tch" or emphatic ch	Sharp "ch" sound
	ble reed shelte	"q" or "ḳ"	Guttural sound
	t of flax	"ḥ" or deep h	Heavy breath sound, common in nam

Note: Some signs have variations or may represent slightly different sounds depending on the time period and dialect. Egyptian writing prioritized *consonants*—vowels were implied by context or left out entirely.

Quick Use Tips:
- Use this list when spelling names or building new words.
- Don't forget to pair with determinatives for clarity.
- Combine with biliterals and triliterals (see Appendix B) for richer writing.

Appendix B: Common Biliteral Sign List

The Egyptian "Two-Letter" Signs – One Symbol, Two Sounds

Sound	Hieroglyph	Glyph Description	Transliteration Notes
pr		House	Appears in "Per-Ra" (House of Ra); a foundational glyph
b³		Human leg walking	Symbol of the *ba* (spiritual soul); used in names and religious texts
dʿ		Cobra and arm (stylized)	Common in verbs meaning "give" or "offer"
ḏt		Cobra with extended hood	Symbolizes "body" or "corpse"; frequent in funerary texts
nf		Snake with raised hood	Appears in the word *nefer* (beautiful); associated with breath or essence
sḫ		Folded cloth and placenta (stylized together)	Root for "remember" or "recall"; abstract concepts
kr		Basket with handle and mouth (merged)	Root for creation, construction, or voice
gr		Hill slope with mouth curve	Often appears in "speak" or "silence" derivatives
jj		Double reed (repeated)	Means "come"; used frequently in narrative and command forms
rʿ		Mouth and arm (stylized sun-disc glyph)	Represents the sun god *Ra*; in divine names
nḥ		Water ripple with twist	"Strong" or "enduring"; used in royal names
sn		Door bolt and water ripple (merged)	Means "brother" or "companion"
qd		Rope coil with bread loaf	Root of words meaning "build" or "construct"
pj		Stool and reed (abbreviated)	Appears in verbs of movement or emergence
ḫt		Placenta and loaf (stylized)	"Thing," "object," or "essence"
ʿn		Arm and water ripple	Root for "life," as in *ankh* (☥)
pḏ		Stool and cobra	"Stretch" or "shoot," often used in reference to arrows
ṯt		Tethering rope (double cross)	Offering or giving symbol in religious contexts

📌 **Notes:**

- **Single signs only**: Each glyph here represents **two consonants** in a single visual unit (no compound clusters).
- Biliteral signs are often followed by **phonetic complements** (uniliteral signs) to reinforce the pronunciation.
- These are the **most common** and practical biliterals for beginners and intermediate readers; more exist in advanced sign lists.

Appendix C: Common Triliteral Sign List

One Symbol, Three Sounds – The Power Glyphs

Sound	Hieroglyph	Glyph Description	Transliteration Notes
nfr		Heart and windpipe	Means "beautiful," "good," or "perfect"; very common
ankh		Loop with cross (Ankh)	Means "life"; appears in blessings, offerings, and amulets
nsw		Reed shelter and throne	"King" or "sovereign"; used in royal titulary
ḫpr		Scarab beetle	Means "become," "transform," or "create"; linked to rebirth
mnḫ		Gaming board or anchor	"Excellent," "effective," "perfect"; often appears in names
ḥtp		Offering table	Means "peace," "offering," or "satisfaction"
sḫm		Scepter with papyrus (merged)	"Power" or "might"; often appears in divine and kingly contexts
ḏsr		Stylized hill or shrine	"Sacred," "holy," or "exalted"; used in temple names
mrj		Hoe + water ripple + arm	Means "to love"; root in personal names like *Meritamun*
ḥḏr		Papyrus stalk + water	"Green," "fresh"; also used symbolically for youth
sbꜣ		Door bolt and star	"Star," "teach," or "learn"; foundational in wisdom texts
rʿw		Sun with rays	Another form of *Ra* (sun deity); alternate writing of "day"
smꜣ		Tied papyrus stalks	"Unite," "bind together"; symbol of unity between Upper and Lower Egypt
wḏꜣ		Papyrus bundle with twisted rope	"Whole," "healthy"; root of "wḏꜣt" (Eye of Horus)
snb		Folded cloth + water + seated man	"Health" or "well-being"; part of standard wish phrases

Appendix D: Transliteration Guide

Turning Glyphs Into Letters (and Back Again)
Transliteration is how Egyptologists convert hieroglyphs into a written form using the Roman alphabet. Since ancient Egyptian didn't write vowels and used a lot of sounds we don't have in English, the transliterations can seem strange at first—but they're easy to learn with this cheat sheet.

Basic Transliteration Key

Symbol	Sound Description	Examples / Notes
ʿ	Glottal stop (like a soft "uh")	Often written with the vulture (🦅)
ꜥ / ʿ	Another glottal stop	Appears in words like "ankh" (life)
ʾ / ꜣ	Slightly different glottal	Used interchangeably with ʿ or ꜥ
A	Implied vowel (not written)	Usually reconstructed based on context
i / y	"ee" or "y" sound	From reed leaf (𓇌); dual role
B	As in "boy"	Foot (𓃀)
P	As in "pet"	Stool (□)
F	As in "fish"	Horned viper (𓆑)
M	As in "moon"	Owl (𓅓)
N	As in "net"	Water ripple (〜)
R	Rolled "r," like in Spanish	Mouth (⌒); often overlaps with "l"
H	Soft "h"	Flax (𓎛)
ḥ	Hard "h" (as in Arabic "ḥ")	Twist of flax (𓎛)
ḫ / kh	Like "ch" in *Bach*	Placenta glyph (⊜)
ẖ	Softer version of "kh"	Less common
S	As in "snake"	Folded cloth (𓋴)
Š	"sh" as in "ship"	Pool glyph (▭)
T	As in "top"	Bread loaf (⌒)
ṯ	"ch" or "tj" sound	Door bolt glyph (⇒)

| D | in "dog" | Hand (⟅) |
| K | d "k" | Basket with handle (⟅) |

Reading Transliteration Like a Pro

Word Example:

nfr → "beautiful, good, perfect"

- n = water
- f = viper
- r = mouth

    (And it might be followed by a seated man determinative if referring to a person)

Name Example:

Tutankhamun → *Twt-ʿnḫ-imn*

- Twt = image
- ʿnḫ = life
- imn = Amun (the god)

Tip: Transliteration isn't pronunciation—just a visual shortcut. Ancient Egyptians would've pronounced things quite differently than we do now.

Using Transliteration in Practice

- Use transliteration to spell names before finding the matching glyphs.
- When looking up glyphs in dictionaries or online tools, search by transliteration.
- Write transliterations under your glyph doodles for clarity.

Quick Transliteration Tips:

- Doubled letters = often plural (e.g., "ss" may indicate repetition or intensity).
- No written vowels? Use "e" to help pronounce unfamiliar words (e.g., "nfr" = "nefer").
- Cartouches usually contain transliterated throne names or birth names in shorthand.

Appendix E: Gardiner's Complete Sign List

The Gardiner Galaxy—How One Egyptologist Cataloged the Code

Imagine if the **Marvel Cinematic Universe** didn't have a guide to track who's who. Tony Stark might get mistaken for Doctor Strange, and Thanos could end up in a rom-com. Now apply that chaos to **Egyptian hieroglyphs**, where there are over **700 unique signs**, some shaped like birds, others like eyes, loaves of bread, or seated gods. Confused yet?
Enter **Sir Alan Gardiner**, the Nick Fury of hieroglyphics.

So Who Was This Gardiner Guy?

Sir Alan Henderson Gardiner (1879–1963) was a British Egyptologist who realized early on that trying to teach or learn hieroglyphics without **a master sign list** was like assembling IKEA furniture with no instruction manual—and all the parts labeled in emojis. A linguistic genius and scholarly powerhouse, Gardiner spent decades immersed in temple walls and dusty papyri, piecing together the ultimate cheat sheet.

And in 1928, he dropped the **Gardiner Sign List**, the most widely-used organizational system for Egyptian hieroglyphs. Basically, the Dewey Decimal System… but for ancient sacred squiggles.

Wait, What Is the Gardiner Sign List?
Think of it as the **Pokédex of Egyptian writing**. It's broken into **26 categories**, labeled A through Z (plus a bonus one called "Aa" for extra weird or rare signs). Each sign is grouped by **what it looks like**, not what it means. So:
- "A" is for **humans** and what humans do.
- "B" is for **human parts** (hands, arms, heads—your average mummy starter pack).
- "G" is for **birds** (because ancient Egypt had *a lot* of birds).
- "R" is for **royal bling**—crowns, scepters, and the "I run this place" accessories.
- "X" is for **bread and cake** (truly, the most delicious category).

Each sign is given a **code**, like A1 (seated man) or R15 (our beloved ꜥ ankh), along with notes on how it's used: phonetically, symbolically, or grammatically.

Why Gardiner's List Is Still the Gold Standard

Yes, it's over 90 years old, and yes, newer sign lists exist with even more glyphs. But Gardiner's is still the go-to for students, scholars, and aspiring glyph geeks like us. Why?
1. **Simplicity** – It gives structure to chaos. You'll never confuse a crocodile (I know, Sobek fans, don't @ me) with a folded cloth again.
2. **Universality** – Egyptologists worldwide use the codes. If you say "Z1" or "M17," they know exactly what you mean. No subtitles needed.
3. **Starter Pack Friendly** – For learners, it's perfect. It doesn't include *every* variation, but it gets you fluent in the basics.

How to Use It Without Losing Your Mind

Let's say you're trying to figure out what a sign that looks like a feather means. Is it part of a costume? Is it a quill? Nope—it's **Ma'at**, goddess of truth, justice, and balance (think ancient Egyptian Wonder Woman). You head to the list and find her in **Category G** (birds) or **Category M** (divine symbols). Boom: you're now reading like a champ.

Or maybe you see a familiar eye symbol. You look it up: it's D4—the **Eye of Horus**. Now you know it's about vision, protection, and divine insight. Bonus points if you've seen *Moon Knight*.

Pop Culture Bonus: It's Basically a Glyph Wiki

If ancient Egypt had the internet, Gardiner's list would be their **Wookieepedia**—the place you go to settle arguments, translate tattoos, or build your own Rosetta Stone replica. Want to know what hieroglyph they used for "beer"? (It's W22, by the way—cheers   ). Gardiner's got your back.

TL;DR — Why This List Rocks

- **It helps organize** an otherwise chaotic writing system.
- **It bridges scholars and learners** with a universal language.
- **It makes translating fun**, like solving a visual crossword puzzle.
- **It's a tool**, not a rulebook. Use it to recognize signs and find patterns.

Final Thought: Use It, Don't Worship It

Sir Gardiner gave us an incredible tool—but it's just that: a tool. Ancient Egyptian writing evolved over thousands of years, with scribes riffing off each other like jazz musicians. So don't be afraid to **doodle with purpose**—use the sign list to learn the rules, then start to play. And if you find a glyph that isn't on the list?

Congrats. You've officially leveled up.

Gardiner's Sign List Categories:

Code Category

Code	Category
A	Man and his occupations
B	Woman and her occupations
C	Anthropomorphic deities
D	Parts of the human body
E	Mammals
F	Parts of mammals
G	Birds
H	Parts of birds
I	Amphibious animals, reptiles, insects
K	Fish and parts of fish
L	Trees and plants
M	Sky, earth, and water
N	Buildings and parts of buildings
O	Vessels of transport
P	Furniture and sacred emblems
Q	Domestic and funerary equipment
R	Temple furniture and sacred emblems
S	Crowns, dress, and staves
T	Warfare, hunting, and butchery
U	Agriculture, crafts, and professions
V	Rope, fiber, baskets, bags, etc.
W	Vessels of stone and earthenware
X	Loaves and cakes
Y	Writings, games, music
Z	Strokes, signs derived from hieratic
Aa	Unclassified signs

Uniliteral Signs with Gardiner Sign Codes
Sound Glyph Gardiner Code Glyph Description

Glyph	Sound	Gardiner Code	Description
𓅐	ꜣ (a)	G1	Vulture (glottal stop or "ah")
𓇋	i / y	M17	Reed leaf
𓂝	ꜥ	D36	Forearm
𓃀	b	D58	Foot

Sound Glyph Gardiner Code Glyph Description

Glyph	Sound	Gardiner Code	Glyph Description
	f	I9	Horned viper
	g	U1	Jar stand or pottery jar
	h	V28	Twisted flax
	ḥ	O4	Reed shelter
	ḫ	Aa1	Placenta or sieve (guttural 'kh')
	ẖ	I10	Belly and udder (deep h-sound)
	ḏ	I10A	Cobra
	d	D46	Hand
	p	Q3	Mat or stool
	s	S29	Folded cloth
	š	N37	Pool or lake
	s	S29	Folded cloth (same as above; often used interchangeably)
	t	X1	Bread loaf
	ṯ	S32	Door bolt
	ṭ	T28	Tethering rope (emphatic 't')
	k	U6	Basket with handle
	g	U1	Jar stand
	m	G17	Owl
	n	N35	Water ripple
	w	G43	Quail chick
	r	D21	Mouth

Notes:

- **Some signs have overlapping forms** (like s/š or t/ṯ) depending on dialect, time period, and regional spelling.
- **Gardiner's codes** help you locate the sign quickly by its shape category (A–Z).
- These 24 signs are the **essential building blocks** of ancient Egyptian writing—you can write almost any Egyptian word using a mix of these and determinatives.

Biliteral Signs with Gardiner Sign Codes

ꜥn	R4	Ankh (life symbol)
ꜥp	G1A	Vulture with curved beak
ḥr	G5	Falcon (Horus)
ḥs	V28 + S29	Twisted flax + cloth
ḥq	S42	Crook/staff of authority
ẖs	Aa1 + S29	Placenta + cloth
ṯn	S32 + N35	Bolt + water ripple
mn	N35 + G1	Water + owl

Sound Glyph		Gardiner Code	Glyph Description
mḥ		G17 + O4	Owl + shelter
mr		G17 + D21	Owl + mouth ("love")
ms		G17 + S29	Owl + cloth ("to be born")
nb		V30	Bowl or basket with handle
nṯ		R8	Axe or flag on pole ("god")
nḥ		N35 + O4	Water ripple + shelter
ns		N35 + S29	Water + cloth
pt		N1	Sky bar with sun
pr		O1	House or building
ra		D21 + N5	Mouth + sun disk
sb		S29 + D58	Cloth + foot ("star")
sn		S29 + N35	Cloth + water ripple ("brother")
st		S29 + X1	Cloth + loaf ("place")
sḫ		S29 + V28	Cloth + flax
sd		S29 + D46	Cloth + hand
sṯ		S29 + S32	Cloth + door bolt
tm		X1 + G17	Loaf + owl
tw		X1 + G43	Loaf + quail chick
wʿ		G43 + G1	Chick + vulture ("one")
wr		G43 + D21	Chick + mouth ("great")
ḫn		I10 + N35	Belly + water ripple

ẖr	I10 + D21	Belly + mouth ("under")
šs	N37 + S29	Lake + cloth

Notes:

- Many biliterals are **combinations of uniliteral signs** you already know.
- Some glyphs appear as **single characters** that contain both consonants (like ⚓ for ʿn).
- Biliterals are crucial for **writing full names and sentences efficiently**.

Triliteral Signs with Gardiner Codes

Sound	Gardiner Code	Glyph Description
ʿḥꜢ	E23	Lion – often symbolic of strength, su or time
ḥtp	R4	Offering table – "peace, offering, satisfaction"
nfr	F35	Heart and trachea – "beautiful, good, perfect"
smr	D21 + G17	Mouth + owl – "companion, friend"

Sound	Gardiner Code	Glyph Description
sbꜣ		Cloth + foot + vulture – "teaching learning"
snb		Cloth + water + foot – "health"

Notes:
- Triliterals are usually followed by **phonetic complements** (uniliteral signs) and **determinatives** to help clarify meaning.
- These glyphs often encapsulate **big concepts** like "life," "god," "beauty," "peace," or names of deities and pharaohs.
- The scarab (🪲 kheper) and offering table (△ hetep) are some of the most **recognizable symbols** of ancient Egypt worldwide.

Common Determinatives in Egyptian Hieroglyphs

	le human or roles	ted man – used for professions, actions, o nouns involving men
	ral humans or lective action	ee seated figures – group or crowd
▭	ions involving the ly	earm – gesture, action, giving

Glyph	...diner e	...ed For	...ph Description
▬		...th, softness, covering	...ded cloth — used in words for clothing, ...ering, concepts
�		...read, binding, repetition	...isted flax — associated with weaving, bindi...
⌷		...ldings, homes	...or plan — "house," "temple," or related ...cept
�◡	+ X1	...stract nouns, concepts	...en used at the end of abstract or complex ...rds
〰		...ter-related meanings	...ple — lake, river, flood, tears
 ▬◡	+ X1	...ace" or location	...pears at the end of names for towns, regio...
⌓		...fering, peace, ...ntentment	...ering table — associated with funerary or ...emonial contexts

How Determinatives Work
- **Clarify meaning**: For example, *nfr* can mean "beautiful," but when followed by a seated

  woman (🧎), it specifically means "beautiful woman."
- **Visual context**: Many different words may sound similar in ancient Egyptian, but their determinatives reveal what kind of word it is.

- **Always come at the end** of the word group or phrase cluster.

💡 Common Ideograms in Egyptian Hieroglyphs

Glyph	Gardiner Code	Word/Idea Represented	Glyph Description
☥	R4	ꜥnḫ ("life")	Ankh – symbol of life and divine energy
𓈗	R8	nṯr ("god")	Axe/flag on a pole – divine presence or deity
🪲	L1	ḫpr ("to become")	Scarab beetle – transformation, rebirth
𓅐	G1	ꜣ ("vulture," also used in names)	Vulture – used in writing words related to mothers or Upper Egypt
𓅓	G17	m ("owl")	Owl – can be both ideogram and phonogram
𓉐	O1	pr ("house")	Floor plan of a house – common in "Per-Ra" (House of Ra)
☐	Q3	p ("mat" or "stool")	Rectangular mat – simple ideogram
☉	N5	Ra ("sun")	Sun disc – represents the sun god Ra and the solar cycle
◁	D21	r ("mouth")	Mouth – idea of speech, name, or command
◠	X1	t ("bread loaf")	Bread – often used to indicate feminine or nourishment
⏚	R4	ḥtp ("offering, peace")	Offering table – idea of satisfaction, funerary peace
👑	F31	sḫm ("power")	Scepter – divine or royal authority
🦵	D58	b ("leg" or "foot")	Leg in walking motion – symbolizes movement, travel
▭	N1	pt ("sky")	Sky symbol with sun – concept of the heavens
◠◠	X1 x2	Dual form (used for "both")	Two bread loaves – indicates duality
𓅓◁𓅱	–	mrw ("love")	Owl + mouth + quail – composite ideogram for affection
▭	Y1	sš ("to write" or "scribe")	Scribal palette – writing and literacy
▭	S32	ṯꜣ ("bolt")	Door bolt – used metaphorically for blocking or closing
〰	N35	n ("water")	Zigzag ripple – water, lake, or flow

Glyph	Gardiner Code	Word/Idea Represented	Glyph Description

Notes:
- **Ideograms are often self-explanatory**, especially in concrete nouns like "sun," "house," or "scarab."
- Some **also function as determinatives or phonograms**, depending on context.
- In many cases, they are used at the **end of a word group** to visually reinforce the meaning.

The Complete Gardiner Sign List – all categories all 700 Glyphs:

NOTE: If Glyph image is missing it is simply due to a lack of available computer files

Gardiner Category A – Man and His Occupations

Glyph	Gardiner Code	Word/Idea Represented	Glyph Description
A1	Seated man	minative)	n, male person
A3	Seated man with stick	minative)	erly man, authority
A5	Seated man with arms raised	minative)	ving, adoration
A10	Standing man with club	minative)	rior, aggression

Sign Glyph Image Description | **Sound / Use** | **Meaning / Notes**

Sign	Glyph	Image Description	Sound / Use	Meaning / Notes
A11		Standing man with arms forward	(determinative)	Offering
A12		Man with arms tied behind	(determinative)	Prisoner, punishment
A13		Man running	(determinative)	Movement, fleeing
A14		Man kneeling with object	(determinative)	Carrying, offering
A15		Man holding papyrus scroll	(determinative)	Scholar, official
A16		Man with sickle	(determinative)	Farmer, harvester
A17		Man with hoe	(determinative)	Agriculture
A18		Man kneeling with hand to mouth	(determinative)	Begging, hunger
A19		Man bowing	(determinative)	Submission, respect
A20		Man with raised fist	(determinative)	Anger, combat
A21		Man holding rope	(determinative)	Captive, restraint

Notes:
- These are **determinative signs**, meaning they are usually placed at the end of a word to indicate **meaning**, not sound.
- Most of them are used to **represent human actions, professions, or status**.

Gardiner Category B – Woman and Her Occupations

Sign	Glyph	Image Description	Sound / Use	Meaning / Notes
B1		Seated woman	(determinative)	Female person; used to mark feminine words and names
B2		Seated woman with child	(determinative)	Motherhood, birth, woman with child
B3		Seated woman with stick	(determinative)	Elderly or noblewoman
B4		Seated woman with hand to mouth	(determinative)	Speaking, eating (feminine)
B5		Seated woman mourning	(determinative)	Lamentation, grief

Sign	Glyph Image	Description	Sound / Use	Meaning / Notes
B6		Standing woman with arms up	(determinative)	Adoration, reverence (feminine)
B7		Standing woman	(determinative)	General female action
B8		Woman with child in arms	(determinative)	Mother and child
B9		Woman giving birth	(determinative)	Fertility, childbirth
B10		Woman kneeling with object	(determinative)	Offering or carrying (female context)
B11		Woman bowing	(determinative)	Submission, respect (feminine)

📝 Usage Notes:
- Like the signs in Category A, most of these are **determinatives**.
- They often appear at the end of words to **denote gender**, **role**, or **activity** specific to women.
- (B1) is the most common glyph for **"woman"** in names (e.g., Nefertiti, Cleopatra).

⛰ Gardiner Category C – Anthropomorphic Deities

Sign	Glyph Image	Description	Sound / Use	Meaning / Notes
C1		Seated god with beard	(determinative)	Generic god or deity; often used after *ntr* (god)
C2		Seated goddess	(determinative)	Female deity; used after goddess names like *Isis*
C3		God with tall crown (Amun-type)	(determinative)	Used for Amun, or gods wearing high plumes
C4		God holding scepter or crook	(determinative)	Deity of rule or power
C5		Goddess with sun disk and horns	(determinative)	Hathor; divine feminine, love, music
C6		God with falcon head (Horus/Ra)	(determinative)	Sky god, protector pharaohs
C7		God with ibis head (Thoth)	(determinative)	Wisdom, writing, moon
C8		God with jackal head (Anubis)	(determinative)	Death, embalming, afterlife
C9		God with crocodile head (Sobek)	(determinative)	Strength, fertility, chaos
C10		Goddess with vulture crown	(determinative)	Often Mut; maternal and protective goddess

C11	God with ram horns	(determin	Khnum or Amun-Ra; creation, ferti
C13	God holding was-scepter ankh	(determin	Symbol of divine power and eternal
C15	Seated god with feather	(determin	Ma'at or gods of justice/order

Usage Notes:
- These signs almost always appear **at the end of a name or phrase involving a deity**, serving as **determinatives**.
- In some cases (like *ntr* for "god"), they follow phonetic glyphs to clarify the word's divine meaning.
- Often paired with symbols like **ankh (♀)**, **was (◭)**, and **djed (𝍤)** in religious inscriptions.

Gardiner Category D — Parts of the Human Body

D1	Eye		ʏe" – used in phrases and deity names (e.g., Ra)
D3	Eyebrow	rminative)	tail in anatomy
D6	Mouth		outh" – used for speaking, verbs, and nan
D8	Teeth	rminative)	ing, biting
D10	Neck and windpipe	rminative)	athing, speaking

Sign	Glyph Image	Description	Sound / Use	Meaning / Notes
D11		Head in profile	(determinative)	Identity, person
D12		Head with beard	*r* (variant)	Ruler, masculine identity
D13		Full face	(determinative)	Facing, orientation
D14		Hair lock	(determinative)	Youth, children
D15		Arm with hand	(determinative)	Action, working
D16		Arm with palm down	(determinative)	Offering, support
D17		Arm with knife	(determinative)	Aggression, butchery
D18		Arm with object	(determinative)	Holding, giving
D19		Arm bent upward	(determinative)	Strength
D20		Palm up	*k^3*	"Ka" – spiritual essence (raised hands)
D21		Hand	*D*	Action, to give
D22		Hand with palm open	(determinative)	Open-handed gesture
D23		Hand holding stick	(determinative)	Holding, possession
D24		Finger	(determinative)	Pointing, detail
D25		Two arms raised	*ḥ^c* (variant)	Praise, joy, greeting
D26		Belly	(determinative)	Body, fullness
D27		Back	(determinative)	Movement, turning
D28		Leg in motion	*ḫ^3*	Movement, action
D29		Leg with foot	(determinative)	Walking, journey
D30		Forearm	' or '	Glottal stop or silent vowel
D31		Arm with rope	(determinative)	Binding, strength

D32	Leg kneeling	rminative)	ɔmission
D36	Toes	rminative)	ps, motion
D40	Hand again (common)		ive," appears in di ankh

Key Notes:
- Many of these are used as **phonograms**, **determinatives**, or both.
- Some (like ⬭, ⬬, and ⬭⬩) are especially important for name writing and verb formation.

Gardiner Category E – Mammals

E1	Foot of an animal	*b*	Common phonogram, also used in w for legs
E3	Goat	(determinativ	Domestic animal; often a sacrifice symł
E7	Cow	(determinativ	Fertility, associated with Hathor
E11	Donkey	(determinativ	Burden-bearing, stubbornness
E14	Hippopotamus lying down	(determinativ	As above, variant pose

Sign	Image Description	Sound / Use	Meaning / Notes
E17	Lion lying down	(determinative)	Protection, repose
E20	Dog	(determinative)	Loyalty, domestic life
E23	Hare or rabbit	*wn*	Used in word for "exist" (*wn*)
E26	Lion's head	(determinative)	Strength, ferocity
E30	Bull's head	(determinative)	Strength, sacred bulls
E34	Monkey's head	(determinative)	Wisdom, mimicry
E38	Lion's mane	(determinative)	Royal strength (decorative use)

Notes:

- Many of these are **determinatives**, meaning they clarify the word's meaning but aren't pronounced.
- A few (like 𓃟, 𓃭, 𓃲) are also **phonograms**, representing sounds or roots in words.

Gardiner Category F – Parts of Mammals

Sign	Image Description	Sound / Use	Meaning / Notes
F2	Horn	(determinative)	Strength, defense

Sign	Glyph Image	Description	Sound / Use	Meaning / Notes
F4		Cow's ear	(determinative)	Hearing, sound
F5		Animal's ear	(determinative)	General listening or auditory meaning
F6		Animal head with neck	(determinative)	Identity or type of animal
F7		Ox head with horns	(determinative)	Fertility, bull cult (e.g., Apis bull)
F8		Lion	L	Used in foreign names, strength
F9		Front part of lion	(determinative)	Used decoratively or for emphasis
F10		Rear part of lion	(determinative)	As above
F11		Lion's tail	(determinative)	May imply action, speed
F12		Animal's tail	(determinative)	Often used symbolically or as adornment
F13		Cow's udder	(determinative)	Fertility, sustenance (linked to Hathor)
F14		Animal leg	K	May appear in words of walking or strength
F15		Animal leg with hoof	(determinative)	Mobility, action
F16		Foreleg of ox	$ḫꜣ$	Meat, sacrifice (often in offering scenes)
F17		Foreleg and thigh	(determinative)	Strength or food offering
F18		Animal hoof	(determinative)	Speed, travel
F19		Ox leg bound	(determinative)	Ritual offering
F20		Heart and windpipe (nfr)	Nfr	"Beautiful," "good," "perfect" – key concept glyph
F21		Windpipe	(determinative)	Breath, speech
F22		Lung	(determinative)	Air, vitality
F23		Liver	(determinative)	Rare; used in anatomy or medical texts
F24		Intestines	(determinative)	Digestion, inner workings
F25		Ox head	(determinative)	Commonly associated with offerings
F26		Bull's tail	(determinative)	Royal adornment, often seen on pharaohs
F27		Skin	(determinative)	Appearance, coverings
F28		Skin with leg	(determinative)	Flayed skin, ritual context
F29		Animal skin tied	(determinative)	Sacrificial imagery
F30		Hair or pelt	(determinative)	Texture, fur

F31	Testicles	determinative)	Fertility, virility
F33	Tail with tuft	determinative)	Often tied to royal or divine symbolism

Key Notes:

- Many signs in this category are used in **sacrificial or anatomical contexts** (offerings, funerary scenes, or divine attributes).

- **F20 (⮾)** is one of the most iconic glyphs in all of Egyptian writing: *nfr* meaning "beautiful" or "perfect."

Gardiner Category G – Birds

G2	Vulture with wings open	(determinative	Divine, protective posture
G4	Kite (bird of prey)	(determinative	Associated with Isis and mourning
G6	Falcon on standard	(determinative	Divine standard, used in religious processions
G8	Owl	*m*	Very common consonant, also means "i or "with"
G10	Owl's head	(determinative	Less frequent

G14	Heron or stork	(determinative	Rare, regional deity use
G16	Duck or pintail	*s³*	Variant bird for son, name elements
G18	Quail chick with wings raised	(determinative	Decorative variant
G20	Swallow	(determinative	Joy, song, freedom
G22	Crested ibis or bustard	(determinative	Rare
G25	Crane	(determinative	Tall wetland bird
G28	Wing	(determinative	Flight, protection
G30	Feather	*m³ˁ*	Truth, Ma'at
G34	Claw or talon	(determinative	Hunting, grasping

Key Highlights:

- **G1 (⚒)** is one of the oldest-used glyphs—often misunderstood as just "a," but really a glottal stop (ˀ).

- **G17 (🦅)** is one of the most frequently used glyphs: the quail chick (*w*).
- **G5 (🦅)** is essential for references to **Horus** and royal legitimacy.

Gardiner Category H – Parts of Birds

Sign	Image Description	nd / Use	Meaning / Notes
H1	Bird wing (extended)	ninative)	it, protection, associated with gods like H(
H4	Two feathers	ninative)	lity, divine presence, associated with Amu
H7	Bird's foot	ninative)	l in context of walking, stepping

Notes:
- These glyphs are **not phonetic**, but are **determinatives**—they give meaning or context to a word.
- **H3 (🦅)** is especially significant: it represents the **feather of Ma'at**, symbolizing truth, justice, and cosmic balance.

Gardiner Category I – Reptiles, Amphibians, and Insects

Sign	Image Description	nd / Use	eaning / Notes
I2	Frog	rminative)	rtility, birth, large numbers
I4	Horned viper		onetic for "f" – common glyph

I6	Cobra with hood flared	(determinative)	protective, uraeus symbolism
I8	Snake coiled	(determinative)	eternity, danger, magical protection
I10	Salamander or lizard	(determinative)	re, used for creeping things
I13	Fly	(determinative)	persistence, annoyance, also military honor in e periods
I16	Two snakes entwined	(determinative)	re magical symbolism

Notes:

- **I4** (⌇) and **I7** ( ) are **frequently used phonetic signs**.
- **I12** the **scarab** is one of the most culturally iconic hieroglyphs, deeply linked with the concept of transformation and rebirth.
- Most other signs are **determinatives**, helping clarify the meaning of a word rather than representing a sound.

Gardiner Category K – Fish and Parts of Fish

K1	Fish (tilapia)	variant)	May represent abundance, Nile life
K3	Fish facing left	(determinative)	Directional or decorative variant
K5	Fish with stripe	(determinative)	Specific identification (e.g. catfish)

K7	Fish (alternate form)	(determinative)	Rebirth or nourishment themes
K9	Fish head	(determinative)	Culinary or offering use

Notes:
- Most signs in Category K are **determinatives**, clarifying meanings related to fishing, food, or the Nile environment.
- Some fish glyphs may be used in magical or ritualistic texts symbolizing **protection** or **nourishment**.

Gardiner Category L – Trees and Plants

L1	Date palm tree	*nḥt*	"Tree" in general; strength, life
L3	Branch with leaves	(determinativ	Fertility, growth
L5	Papyrus stem	*wȝḏ* (variant)	Often in names, rebirth
L8	Papyrus plant	(determinativ	Lower Egypt emblem
L10	Reeds or sedge	*nsw* (part)	Associated with royalty (used in "king" *nswt*)
L12	Plant with curved stalk	(determinativ	Specific flora; fertility

Sign	Glyph Image	Description	Sound / Use	Meaning / Notes
L13		Leaf	(determinative)	Fragility, detail
L14		Lotus flower	*sšn*	Upper Egypt symbol; rebirth, sun, purity
L15		Lotus in bloom	(determinative)	Same as above, decorative use
L16		Lotus with stem and buds	(determinative)	Rebirth, decoration, festivals
L17		Lotus + papyrus combination	(determinative)	Unification of Upper and Lower Egypt
L18		Bundle of plants	(determinative)	Offering, agriculture
L19		Tree trunk	(determinative)	Stability, construction
L20		Tree	(determinative)	Life, nature, shade
L21		Tree with branches	(determinative)	Sacred tree or specific species
L22		Tree with hanging fruit	(determinative)	Fertility, food
L23		Vine or grape cluster	*irp*	Wine, celebration
L24		Vine with trellis	(determinative)	Growth, agriculture
L25		Olive or similar fruit tree	(determinative)	Oil, healing
L26		Shrub or bush	(determinative)	Wild growth, nature
L27		Bundle of herbs or reeds	(determinative)	Medicine, fragrance
L28		Grain stalk	*šmꜥ*	Barley or emmer wheat (symbol of food, offering)
L29		Wheat ear	*ḥꜣt*	Bread, agriculture
L30		Wheat sheaf	(determinative)	Harvest, provision
L31		Reed leaf	*i / y*	Common phonogram for "i" or "y"
L32		Curved reed or sedge	(determinative)	Decoration, writing tools
L33		Plant on stand or basket	(determinative)	Temple offerings

Sign	Glyph Image	Description	Sound / Use	Meaning / Notes
L34		Garlands or wreaths	(determinative)	Celebration, decoration
L35		Stalk tied in loop	(determinative)	Binding, unity

🌑 Gardiner Category M – Sky, Earth, and Water

Sign	Glyph Image	Description	Sound / Use	Meaning / Notes
M1		Reed leaf	i / y	Common uniliteral sign; vowel or consonant use
M2		Sky bar with sun	pt	"Sky"; often appears in cosmology and temple writing
M3		Star	(determinative)	Night, sky, heavens
M4		Star with rays	(determinative)	Light, divine source
M5		Moon crescent	(determinative)	Lunar deity, time
M6		Moon with full disk	(determinative)	Time cycles, month
M7		Cloud with rain	(determinative)	Storms, water from sky
M8		Lightning bolt	(determinative)	Sudden power, deity wrath
M9		Wind symbol	(determinative)	Air, breath, movement
M10		Horizon with sun rising	$ꜣẖt$	"Akhet" = horizon; rebirth, solar imagery
M11		Horizon with two peaks	(determinative)	Duality, balance
M12		Mountain triple peak	$ḳꜣ$	"Mountain"; can represent foreign lands
M13		Earth line or plain	$tꜣ$	"Land"; Egypt itself often written with this
M14		Field or flat plain	(determinative)	Geography, agriculture
M15		Hill or desert dune	$dšr.t$ (red land)	"Desert"; chaos, wild space
M16		Mound with plants	(determinative)	Fertile land, sown field
M17		Water ripple	N	Common uniliteral sign for "n"

M18	Water pool		sed in many water-based terms
M20	Wave symbol	terminative)	ea, flood
M22	Bucket pouring water	terminative)	Offering, libation
M24	Container of water	terminative)	urity, rituals
M26	Nile flood lines	terminative)	nundation, agriculture
M29	Mud with plants	terminative)	ertility, creation (associated with Khnum)

Notes:

- (M1) and (M17) are **core uniliteral phonograms**.
- **M10 ( )** "Akhet" is a key symbol in Egyptian cosmology and temple names.
- These signs appear frequently in writing about **geography, seasons, deities, and rituals**.

Gardiner Category N – Buildings and Architecture

N1	Plan view of house	r	"House"; core glyph for *Per* (temple, fam estate)

Sign	Glyph Image	Description	Sound / Use	Meaning / Notes
N5		Reed shelter or shrine	ḥ	"House," often as a prefix (ḥwt-nṯr = "temple of god")
N6		Building with door	(determinative)	Entry, threshold
N7		Double doors	sḫn	Often symbolic of separation or entry into sacred space
N8		Door bolt	s or tch	Sound value for tch or as determinative for doors
N9		Window	(determinative)	Vision, access
N10		Column	(determinative)	Strength, support
N11		Column with capital	(determinative)	Lotus or papyrus capital; royal and temple architecture
N12		Wall	(determinative)	Protection, enclosure
N13		Enclosure wall	(determinative)	Fortifications, palace
N14		Arch or curved roof	(determinative)	Tomb, canopy
N15		Stepped structure	ḥsb (rare)	Counting house, administration
N16		Staircase	(determinative)	Movement, elevation
N17		Slope or ramp	(determinative)	Access, labor
N18		Doorframe	(determinative)	Passage, transition
N19		Gate or portal	(determinative)	Entrance, celestial doorway
N20		Fortress or castle	ḥwt (variant)	Defense, rulership
N21		Pyramid	mr	Tomb of a king, literal and symbolic use
N22		House with offering platform	(determinative)	Residence of priesthood or ritual space
N23		Gate flanked by towers	(determinative)	Fortified entry, royal gates
N24		Treasury or granary	(determinative)	Storage, wealth, prosperity
N25		House with offerings inside	(determinative)	Mortuary chapel, shrine

N26	Storage jar inside house	(determinative)	Provisions, household
N28	Workshop or mill	(determinative)	Work, craftsmanship

Notes:

- **N1 (□)** is one of the most foundational glyphs in the script, meaning "house," and used across names and place words.
- Many glyphs in this category function as **determinatives** for words related to **architecture, ritual spaces, or home life**.

Gardiner Category O – Vessels of Transport (Boats, Ships, and Vehicles)

O1	Boat or ship (simple hull)	*t*	Generic "boat"; key glyph for transport, funerary barque
O3	Ship with sail	(determinative)	Seafaring, foreign travel
O5	Boat with shrine	(determinative)	Funerary barque of gods or kings
O7	Boat carrying obelisk	(determinative)	Heavy transport, royal construction
O9	Warship with high prow	(determinative)	Military symbolism

Sign	Image Description	Sound / Use	Meaning / Notes
O13	Sacred boat on platform	(determinative)	Seen in temple carvings; symbol of divine journey
O15	Obelisk on boat	(determinative)	Transport of sacred items
O17	Wagon or ox-cart	(determinative)	Land travel (rare)
O20	Royal litter or sedan chair	(determinative)	Nobility, ceremony

Notes:

- **O (___)** is a key glyph meaning "boat" (*dpt*), found in many royal and funerary texts.
- Many glyphs here are **determinatives**, clarifying context for travel, water, royal processions, or sacred journeys.
- Boats were central to Egyptian cosmology, particularly in the **solar journey of Ra** and funerary rites.

Gardiner Category P – Domestic and Funerary Furniture

Sign	Image Description	Sound / Use	Meaning / Notes
P5	Bed or sleeping platform	(determinative)	Rest, dreams, protection
P7	Headrest with support	(determinative)	Stability; transitional symbol in tombs

P8	Footstool	determinative)	Subordination, support
P10	Box or chest	determinative)	Storage, offerings
P12	Offering table with loaves	determinative)	Seen in "ḥtp-di-nsw" ("an offering which king gives")
P14	Basin or foot-wash bowl	determinative)	Purification, ablution
P16	Censer (incense burner)	determinative)	Worship, smoke offerings
P19	Table with jug or cup	determinative)	Drinking, banquet, libation

Notes:

- **P1 (ᗡ)** is both a **phonogram** (*p*) and a **determinative** for stools or seats.
- Many of these signs appear in **offering formulas**, funerary texts, or **tomb inscriptions** depicting daily life or ritual provision.
- **P11 (⌐⊨)** and **P12 (⍭)** are particularly important in writing **"ḥtp-di-nsw"** ("an offering which the king gives…").

Gardiner Category Q – Temple Furniture and Sacred Emblems

Q3	Standard with falcon	(determinati·	Horus; divine kingship
Q5	Standard with ibis head	(determinati·	Thoth; writing, wisdom
Q7	Standard with crescent & disc	(determinati·	Moon god Khonsu
Q9	Standard with lotus	(determinati·	Symbol of Upper Egypt
Q11	Shrine with open doors	(determinati·	Access to deity; sacred enclosure
Q14	Sphinx or recumbent lion	(determinati·	Divine guardian, royal power
Q16	Emblem with dual feathers	(determinati·	Represents dual gods, balance
Q18	Emblem of scepter & feather	(determinati·	Authority and truth
Q20	Sacred flag	(determinati·	Temple boundary or divine announcer

Notes:
- These glyphs are primarily **determinatives or ideograms**, used in religious, **temple, or ceremonial inscriptions**.
- Many represent **deities, nome (regional) standards**, or **sacred objects** carried in **ritual processions**.

- **Q13 ( )**, the **winged sun disk**, is among the most powerful protection symbols in all of Egyptian art.

Gardiner Category R – Crowns, Dress, Staves, and Scepters

Sign	Glyph Image	Description	Sound / Use	Meaning / Notes
R1		White Crown of Upper Egypt	$ḥḏt$	Worn by southern kings; seen in royal imagery
R2		Red Crown of Lower Egypt	$dšrt$	Worn by northern kings; represents the delta
R3		Double Crown (Pschent)	$sḥmty$	Unified crown of Upper and Lower Egypt
R4		Blue Crown (Khepresh)	(determinative)	Military or ceremonial crown
R5		Nemes headcloth	(determinative)	Worn by pharaohs; associated with kingship
R6		Royal uraeus (cobra)	(determinative)	Protective crown element; Wadjet goddess
R7		Wig or headdress	(determinative)	Nobility, deity, ritual attire
R8		Lock of youth (sidelock)	(determinative)	Indicates youth or prince
R9		Apron	(determinative)	Garment of officials and gods
R10		Robe or cloak	(determinative)	Priesthood or formality
R11		Sandals	$sk̲$	Daily wear, journeys, ritual use
R12		Crook	$ḥqꜣ$	Symbol of rulership; held by gods and pharaohs
R13		Flail	$nḫꜣk$ (rare)	Authority, agriculture, often paired with crook
R14		Scepter	$wꜣs$	Power, divine control
R15		Ankh (☥)	$ꜥnḫ$	"Life"; iconic symbol of eternal life
R16		Djed pillar	$ḏd$	Stability, Osiris, resurrection
R17		Scepter with papyrus	(determinative)	Youth, Lower Egypt
R18		Scepter with lotus	(determinative)	Upper Egypt, fertility

R19	Heqa-scepter with flail	(determinati·	Royal regalia combination
R21	Fan or ceremonial flabellum	(determinati·	Temple ritual, royal procession
R23	Mirror	$ḥ't$	Beauty, clarity, sacred reflection
R25	Sistrum rattle	$sšš$ (rare)	Sacred music, goddess Hathor
R27	Cowl or headband	(determinati·	Royalty, ceremonial dress

Notes:
- **R1–R3**: Crown glyphs are key to identifying **royal status** and **geopolitical symbolism**.
- **R15 (☥)** Ankh, **R16 (꒫)** Djed, and **R14 (꜔)** Was-scepter are part of the **divine triad of power, life, and stability**.
- Many signs in this category are used in **funerary contexts**, **ritual processions**, and **royal titulary**.

Gardiner Category S – Warfare, Hunting, and Butchery

S2	Mace	leterminative)	Weapon; associated with smiting enemies power
S4	Club or cudgel	leterminative)	Close combat, physical force
S6	Spear and shield	leterminative)	Defense, battle

S7	Bow	ỉ	Hunting, archery, determinative for foreign enemies
S9	Axe with curved blade	leterminative)	Butchery, labor
S11	Sling or slingshot	leterminative)	Hunting; often in youth or mythological scenes
S13	Butcher's knife	leterminative)	Ritual slaughter or meat preparation
S15	Flaying knife	leterminative)	Skinning, sacrifice
S18	Captive man with hands tied	leterminative)	Enemy of the state or defeated foe
S20	Enemies with heads down	leterminative)	Group of prisoners or subdued population
S22	Pile of phalluses (trophy)	leterminative)	Also used to count enemy losses; controversial glyph
S24	Bound animal or enemy	leterminative)	Subjugation or tribute scene

Notes:
- This is one of the most **visually dramatic** categories, often seen in **battle scenes, tomb reliefs**, or inscriptions describing pharaohs' conquests.

- Several signs (S18–S24) are **used to represent enemies**, especially in temple inscriptions celebrating victory over foreign lands.

Gardiner Category T – Agriculture, Crafts, and Professions

Sign	Glyph Image	Description	Sound / Use	Meaning / Notes
T1		Plow	(determinative)	Agriculture, cultivation
T2		Hoe	*mr*	Used in "love" (*mr*), cultivation
T3		Sickle or reaping hook	(determinative)	Harvesting crops
T4		Forked stick (digging tool)	(determinative)	Fieldwork, agriculture
T5		Pickaxe or adze	$ḥbs$ (rare)	Digging or woodworking
T6		Mallet or hammer	(determinative)	Crafting, shaping stone
T7		Adze	*msk*	Symbol of rebirth; used in "Opening of the Mouth" ritual
T8		Carpenter's square	(determinative)	Measurement, precision
T9		Trowel or scraper	(determinative)	Construction, craft
T10		Saw or blade	(determinative)	Wood or stone working
T11		Grindstone or mortar	(determinative)	Grinding grain, food prep
T12		Millstone or grinding slab	(determinative)	Agriculture, bread-making
T13		Basket with handle	*k*	Common uniliteral "k" sound; also used as determinative
T14		Mat-maker's knife	(determinative)	Textile or craft work
T15		Basket with cloth	(determinative)	Offering, gathering
T16		Pottery wheel	(determinative)	Ceramic work
T17		Potter's kiln or oven	(determinative)	Cooking or baking
T18		Smith's bellows	(determinative)	Metalworking, fire
T19		Anvil	(determinative)	Forging, tools

T20	Leather worker's knife	(determinative	Skinning, tanning
T22	Loom or weaving frame	(determinative	Textile manufacture
T24	Ladder or scaffold	(determinative	Elevation, construction
T26	Plumb bob or weight	(determinative	Alignment, architecture
T28	Table for offerings or labor	(determinative	Ritual or daily provision

Notes:
- These glyphs appear in **craftsmen scenes**, **daily life depictions**, and **titles of professions**.
- **T2** (𓌳) is important for both agriculture and symbolic terms like "love" (*mr*).
- **T7** (𓌢) and **T18** (𓌉) show the **religious and industrial depth** of Egyptian society—ranging from sacred rites to blacksmithing.

Gardiner Category U – Rope, Fiber, Baskets, and Bags

U2	Loop of rope or cord	determinative)	Binding, fastening
U4	Rope with knot	determinative)	Binding, unity, covenant
U6	Strap or loop with handle	determinative)	Carrying or lifting tools

Sign	Image Description	Sound / Use	Meaning / Notes
U7	Basket (without handle)	? (variant)	Often seen in "household" words or determinatives
U9	Wide basket	determinative)	Containment, storage
U11	Bag or pouch	determinative)	Wealth, sacred item, priestly use
U13	Braided rope	determinative)	Strength, unity, teamwork
U15	Papyrus rope tied	determinative)	Unity, ritual tying, temple use

Notes:
- Several of these glyphs (**U1, U3, U8**) serve as both **phonograms** and **determinatives**, making them versatile.
- Baskets and rope are key in **offering scenes**, **daily life**, and **religious symbolism**, representing containment, order, and connection.
- **U8 (⚐)** is especially significant—it appears in royal names like *Neb-kheperu-ra* ("Lord of the manifestations of Ra").

Gardiner Category V – Stone and Pottery Vessels

Sign	Image Description	nd / Use	Meaning / Notes
V2	Tall jar with flared top	:erminative)	sed in offering or libation scenes

V6	Round-bottom pot	terminative)	ater or oil; temple use
V8	Large basin	terminative)	ashing, libation, purification
V10	Small jar or flask	terminative)	ften labeled as ointment or perfume vess
V12	Squat jar	terminative)	eneral storage or food container
V14	Tall conical jar	terminative)	torage, symbolic abundance
V17	Jug with long neck	terminative)	live oil, anointing purposes
V19	Container on pedestal	terminative)	ffering vessel in elite or divine contexts

Notes:

- Many of these glyphs are **determinatives** associated with **food, drink, ritual offerings**, and **household storage**.
- **V1 ()** is a **phonogram** used for the sound *ḏ* (as in "djedi").
- **V3 ()** literally spells *ḥnqt*, the ancient word for "beer," a daily staple and offering item.

Gardiner Category W – Metal Vessels and Miscellaneous Containers

Sign	Glyph	Image Description	Sound / Use	Meaning / Notes
W1		Bowl with spout (metal or stone)	*nw*	"Pot" or "vessel"; appears in offering lists and daily life
W2		Cup or chalice with stem	(determinative)	Ritual drink, sacred offering
W3		Container with horizontal lid	(determinative)	Food container, often seen in tombs
W4		Squat bowl with cover	(determinative)	Storage of sacred or domestic items
W5		Basin with legs	(determinative)	Used in purification or footwashing rituals
W6		Container on brazier	(determinative)	Cooking or heating in rituals
W7		Bowl with incense or fire	(determinative)	Sacred fire, purification, worship
W8		Pot with tilting lid	(determinative)	Used to denote pouring or spilling
W9		Lidded vase with decorations	(determinative)	Funerary urn, sacred usage
W10		Slender metal vessel	(determinative)	Oil, perfume, or sacred anointing liquids
W11		Tubular vessel with flame	(determinative)	Oil lamp or ceremonial fire
W12		Jar on stand	(determinative)	Offering, temple ritual
W13		Flask or bottle with stopper	(determinative)	Sealed container, sacred liquid
W14		Rounded metal jar	(determinative)	General container for storage
W15		Pot set inside another	(determinative)	Nesting containers, abundance
W16		Container suspended by rope	(determinative)	Transport, portability
W17		Jar with stylized handles	(determinative)	Often decorative or elite usage
W18		Long-handled ladle or spoon	(determinative)	Food or offering ritual
W19		Spouted metal vessel	(determinative)	Pouring water, libation
W20		Vessel on wheels or cart	(determinative)	Transporting sacred materials
W21		Container with rope or cloth	(determinative)	Protective covering, burial

| W22 | Jug with string or stopper | (determinativ | Tied container, preservation |

| W24 | Elaborate ceremonial container | (determinativ | Elite temple use or high ritual |

Notes:

- Many glyphs in Category W are **determinatives**, showing the material (often metal), **function**, or **ritual importance** of a vessel.

- **W1 (𓏏𓏏𓏏)** is one of the most common, seen in texts that list **offerings** or household goods.

Gardiner Category X – Loaves and Cakes

| X2 | Flat bread or cake | determinative) Food offering or sustenance |

| X4 | Triangular cake or wedge | determinative) Baked goods, ritual food |

| X6 | Bread with central line | determinative) May denote special or elite food |

| X9 | Round cake on a stand | determinative) Elevated or sacred offering |

| X11 | Conical loaf | determinative) May reference barley or emmer |

Notes:

- **X1 (⌒)** is extremely common—it's both a **uniliteral** for the sound "t" and a **feminine marker** in grammar.
- These glyphs frequently appear in **offering formulas**, such as in tomb inscriptions: "Bread, , oxen, fowl…"

♪♪ **Gardiner Category Y – Writing, Games, Music**

Y2	Ink pot and pens	(determinativ	Writing, learning, administration
Y4	Open papyrus scroll	(determinativ	Reading, knowledge
Y6	Tally stick or counting marker	(determinativ	Arithmetic, records
Y8	Game pieces or counters	(determinativ	Board games, divination
Y13	Sistrum (ritual rattle)	ꜣšš	Sacred sound, goddess Hathor

Notes:

- Y1 (⌒) is one of the most iconic glyphs in the entire system, representing the scribe's toolkit.

- Y3 (⌒) is used in the word *mḏꜣt*, meaning "book" or "sacred text".
- Game

- and music symbols (Y7–Y14) are often used in tomb scenes to illustrate joy, status, or the journey to the afterlife.

Gardiner Category Z – Strokes, Hieratic-Derived, Geometric Figures

Z1	Three vertical strokes	lural)	Indicates plural when placed after noun or adjective
Z3	One diagonal stroke	ingular/endi	Used for marking singular; someti a grammatical marker
Z5	Group of dots	eterminative	Often symbolic or abstract plural
Z10	Crossed lines or asterisk shape	eterminative	Can indicate multiplicity, magic, o emphasis
Z12	Broken stroke or angled line	eterminative	Stylized punctuation or separator
Z14	Complex hieratic mark	eterminative	Rare; often in religious or high-lev inscriptions

Notes:
- The Z-category signs are primarily grammatical, structural, or stylistic markers.
- Z1 (I) is extremely common and one of the most important determinatives, denoting plurality.
- These glyphs often derive from hieratic script and may not represent objects but rather serve to clarify grammar or formatting.

:

Gardiner Category Aa – Unclassified or Rare Signs

This section includes hieroglyphs that don't fit into the A–Z categories. These are rare, obscure, or unusual glyphs, often used only in very specific words, names, or time periods.

Aa4	Animal tail	(determinativ	Associated with ceremonial costun or deities
Aa6	Phallus	(determinativ	Fertility, creation, sometimes anatomical context
Aa8	Abstract spiral shape	(determinativ	Rare; possibly magical or decorativ
Aa10	Abstract hair or fiber	(determinativ	Often appears with grooming item priestly tools
Aa12	Simplified "ab" (heart) glyph	*jb* (variant)	Emotional/spiritual center, less for variant
Aa14	Alternate form of twisted flax	*ḥ*	Variant of the standard twisted flax sign (H-sound)
Aa17	Short stroke with tail	(determinativ	Seen in Old Kingdom or niche text
Aa19	Stretched hide or leather	(determinativ	Used in texts related to crafts, tann or preparation

Notes:

- Aa-category signs are largely determinatives, often with uncertain or obscure meanings.
- Some are variant forms of common glyphs or symbolic/ritual representations.
- These are rarely used outside of specific religious, funerary, or magical texts

Appendix F: Further Reading and Resources

Keep Learning, Creating, and Connecting

Books (Beginner to Intermediate)

1. *How to Read Egyptian Hieroglyphs*
By Mark Collier and Bill Manley
A classic starter guide with clear lessons, visuals, and accessible language. Structured like a workbook.

2. *Egyptian Grammar: Being an Introduction to the Study of Hieroglyphs*
By Sir Alan Gardiner
The OG manual of Middle Egyptian—detailed and scholarly. Best for intermediate learners.

3. *Middle Egyptian: An Introduction to the Language and Culture of Hieroglyphs*
By James Peter Allen
A comprehensive but approachable college-level textbook on Middle Egyptian.

4. *Reading Egyptian Art*
By Richard H. Wilkinson
Focuses on interpreting symbols and meanings, rather than language mechanics.

5. *The Hieroglyphs Handbook*
By Philip Ardagh and Illustrated by Sue Michniewicz
A light, colorful introduction great for students, artists, or casual learners.

Academic and Online Tools

1. JSesh Hieroglyphic Text Editor

   - https://jsesh.qenherkhopeshef.org
     Free professional software for typing and formatting hieroglyphs. Great for layout and learning glyph codes.

2. UCLA's Digital Karnak

   - http://dlib.etc.ucla.edu/projects/Karnak
     Explore a digital recreation of one of Egypt's greatest temple complexes.

3. Thesaurus Linguae Aegyptiae (TLA)

- https://aaew.bbaw.de/tla
  A massive academic database of Egyptian texts and translations (with search by transliteration).

4. MET Museum's Digital Catalogs

- https://www.metmuseum.org
  Search for hieroglyph-covered artifacts and browse scholarly documentation and high-res imagery.

Creative & Visual Inspiration

1. Ancient Egypt Coloring Book
Great for practicing drawing and decorating glyphs while learning vocabulary and patterns.

2. Egyptian Mythology Comics (Webtoon / Indie)
Search for artist reinterpretations of Egyptian myths—perfect for visual learners and storytellers.

3. Pinterest & Instagram Art Tags

- #hieroglyphics
- #egyptianart
- #doodlingwithpurpose
  Follow artists and educators sharing glyph-inspired creations, tattoos, notebooks, and scroll art.

Fun & Games

1. *Assassin's Creed: Origins* (Discovery Tour Mode)
Explore real hieroglyphic sites in-game with guided historical facts.

2. *Sphinx and the Cursed Mummy*
An older, underrated game with real mythological references and glyph decoding elements.

3. Hieroglyph Keyboard Apps & Fonts
Try mobile apps that let you write your name in glyphs or use free hieroglyphic fonts in your digital designs.

Where to Go (in the real world!)

- The British Museum (London) – Home of the Rosetta Stone
- The Met (NYC) – Extensive Egyptian wing with sarcophagi, stelae, and scrolls
- The Louvre (Paris) – Massive Egyptian collection
- Field Museum (Chicago) – Hands-on Egypt exhibit with hieroglyph learning stations
- Egyptian Museum (Cairo) – The holy grail of ancient Egyptian artifacts

Dream Trip Tip: Visiting Egypt? Check out guided temple tours in Luxor, Aswan, and Giza that focus on inscriptions and their meanings. An be sure to hit the isle of Philae. My personal favorite spot!

Recommended YouTube Channels

• Doodling with Purpose *(That's us!)*
Your go-to video companion for learning glyphs step-by-step, with clear visuals and fun commentary.

• Scribe of Thoth
Focuses on mythology, script, and history.

• World Museum Tours
High-res walk-throughs of Egyptian galleries and ruins.

You're not just doodling—you're reviving a language that once held the voice of gods and kings. That deserves a little reverence, even when done casually.

Appendix G: Glossary of Terms

Speak Like a Scribe

A–C

Ankh (☥) – A hieroglyph meaning "life," often shown being offered by gods to pharaohs. One of the most iconic symbols of ancient Egypt.

Bilateral Sign – A hieroglyph that represents two consonant sounds (e.g., *pr* for "house").

Cartouche – An oval shape enclosing a royal or divine name. Symbolically protects the name and grants it immortality.

Determinative – A non-phonetic sign placed at the end of a word to clarify its meaning (e.g., seated man = person; house = place).

Djed ( ) – A pillar-like glyph symbolizing stability and strength. Associated with Osiris.

Doodling with Purpose – The practice of learning while sketching; in this book, using hieroglyphs as both visual and educational tools.

F–H

Falcon ( ) – Symbol of the god Horus; represents protection, vision, and royalty.

Glyph – A single character in hieroglyphic writing; can be a letter, sound, word, or symbol.

Heka – Ancient Egyptian term for "magic" or "divine speech," believed to be activated through writing and ritual.

Hieratic – A cursive version of hieroglyphs used for papyrus and daily writing by scribes.

Hieroglyph – From Greek for "sacred carving," this term refers to the symbolic writing system of ancient Egypt.

I–M

Ideogram – A glyph that represents both a concept and its sound (e.g.,   for "Ra," meaning both the sun and the god).

Ka – A spiritual aspect of the self; a person's life force or soul.

Ma'at ( ) – The concept of truth, justice, and cosmic balance, personified as a goddess with a feather.

Medu Netjer – The Egyptian term for hieroglyphic writing; translates as "words of the gods."

Middle Egyptian – The classical form of the Egyptian language, most commonly taught to students and used in temples and tombs.

N–R

Neter ( ) – A glyph for "god" or "divine being"; often stylized like a flag or pole.

Peret – One of the three Egyptian seasons; the "growing season" (October to February).

Phonetic Complement – A uniliteral glyph added after a biliteral or triliteral to reinforce pronunciation.

Rosetta Stone – The key to deciphering Egyptian hieroglyphs. Contains the same text in Greek, Demotic, and Hieroglyphic scripts.

S–Z

Scarab (🪲) – A beetle glyph representing rebirth, transformation, and the god Khepri.

Scribe – A trained writer and record keeper. In Egypt, scribes were highly respected and essential to administration and religion.

Sed Festival – A royal celebration of a pharaoh's continued strength and authority, held after 30 years of rule.

Season (Akhet, Peret, Shemu) – The Egyptian year was divided into three 4-month seasons tied to the Nile: Flood (Akhet), Growth (Peret), Harvest (Shemu).

Shemu – The dry or harvest season in the Egyptian calendar (February to June).

Triliteral Sign – A glyph that represents three consonant sounds (e.g., *nfr* for "beautiful").

Tutankhamun – A famous young pharaoh of the 18th dynasty; name means "Living image of Amun."

Uniliteral Sign – A glyph representing a single consonant. The building blocks of most hieroglyphic writing.

Wepet Renpet – Egyptian New Year's Day, marked by the heliacal rising of the star Sirius.

Appendix H: Exercise Answers and Key

Chapter 7 – Biliterals & Triliterals Practice
"Per-Ra" (House of Ra)

- ▭ (pr) = "house"

- ⌒ + ☉ = "Ra" (mouth + sun disk)

This would appear as:

→ ▭ ⌒ ☉

Chapter 8 – Determinative Exercise

(m) + (s) + (s) + (seated man)
= *mss* + determinative → "Moses" or "born of," with a personal noun determinative
If the determinative were   instead of   , it might shift the meaning toward a place or institution.

Chapter 10 – Sentence Structure Practice
"The king gives bread."
→ *di nswt t*

- ⌒ (Hand) = di ("gives")

- ⌒⌒ (Crowned seated man) = nswt ("king")

- ⌒ (Bread loaf) = t

Arranged: verb → subject → object

⌒ ⌒⌒⌒
→ di nswt t = "The king gives bread"

Chapter 12 – Layout Exercise
Vertical Layout:
scss
CopyEdit

- ♀ (**ankh**) → ☥

- (**nswt**, "king") → ⌒⌒ or

- ⌒ (**t**, "bread") → already a proper hieroglyph

Final line in glyphs only:

☥ ⌒⌒ ⌒

Direction: Read top to bottom. Faces (if present) face left or right to guide full direction. Keep glyphs balanced visually in a block layout.

Chapter 13 – Cartouche Construction
Tutankhamun = *Twt-ꜥnḫ-imn*

- Image (⬭), life (☥), god Amun (🐦〰)

These would be wrapped inside an oval cartouche (long horizontal or vertical). Line at the base = grounded royal name.

Chapter 14 – Phrase Practice
"An offering that the king gives: life, prosperity, and health" → *hetep di nswt: ankh, wedja, seneb*
Glyphs:

- ◿ = *hetep* → "offering table"

- ⬭ = *di* → "hand" (to give)

- 〰𓇋𓊪 = *nswt* → "king"

- ☥ = *ankh* → "life"

- 🐍 = *wedja* → "prosperity, protection"

- ⋀ = *seneb* → "health"

Full offering phrase in hieroglyphs:

◿ ⬭ 〰𓇋𓊪 ☥ 🐍 ⋀

Which reads:
"An offering that the king gives: life, prosperity, and health."

Chapter 15 – Birthday Dating Practice
Example:
Year 7, Month 2 of Peret, Day 12 of Beyoncé I

- ⊙ + ⫶ (7 strokes)
- Glyph for "Peret" season (growing fields)
- Month 2 and Day 12 with number glyphs
- Beyoncé's name in a custom cartouche

Chapter 10 – Room Labeling Example
Label: "Bed" → no direct glyph, but use:

- ⬭🕱 (loaf + shelter or bed frame)

- Add determinative for object (rectangle with line)
  You can create composite "home" glyph clusters using pr (house), nht (wood/tree), etc.

Chapter 16 – Inscription Translation

⬭ ﹏𝕀𝕭◠ ☥ ◠ ⊏◻o

- ⬭ = *di* ("to give" – hand)

- ﹏𝕀𝕭◠ = *nswt* ("king" – crowned seated figure)

- ☥ = *ankh* ("life" – cross with loop)

- ◠ = *t* ("bread" – bread loaf)

- ⊏◻o = *hnqt* ("beer" – jug and determinative)

Chapter 17 – Translating Real Inscriptions

Original: ☥
Transliteration: *di nswt ankh irt djed pr z*

Hieroglyphic version:

⬭ ﹏𝕀𝕭◠ ☥ ◠ 𝕝 ◻ 𝕱

- ⬭ = *di* ("to give" – hand)

- ﹏𝕀𝕭◠ = *nswt* ("king" – crowned seated figure)

- ☥ = *ankh* ("life")

- ◠ = *irt* ("eye" – Eye of Horus)

- 𝕝 = *djed* ("protection" – cobra or pillar)

- ◻ = *pr* ("house" – rectangular house glyph)

- 𝕱 = *z* ("man/person" – seated figure)

Chapter 18– Symbolic Sentence

"Truth is balance."

→ *ma'at is hetep*

- (feather of Ma'at)

- Glyph for offering/peace (⬠)

Decorate with symmetrical layout, balance lines, or sun rays to enhance sacred tone.

Chapter 19 – Glyph Journal Example
Emotion Tracker:

☥ = Feeling alive (*Ankh – life*)

〰 = Emotional tide (*Water ripple – mw*)

🪲 = Transformation phase (*Scarab – kheper*)

🐍 = Defensive (*Cobra – djed*)

𝄽 = Balanced (*Feather – ma'at*)Use small glyph boxes, colored pencil, or watercolor to illustrate these.

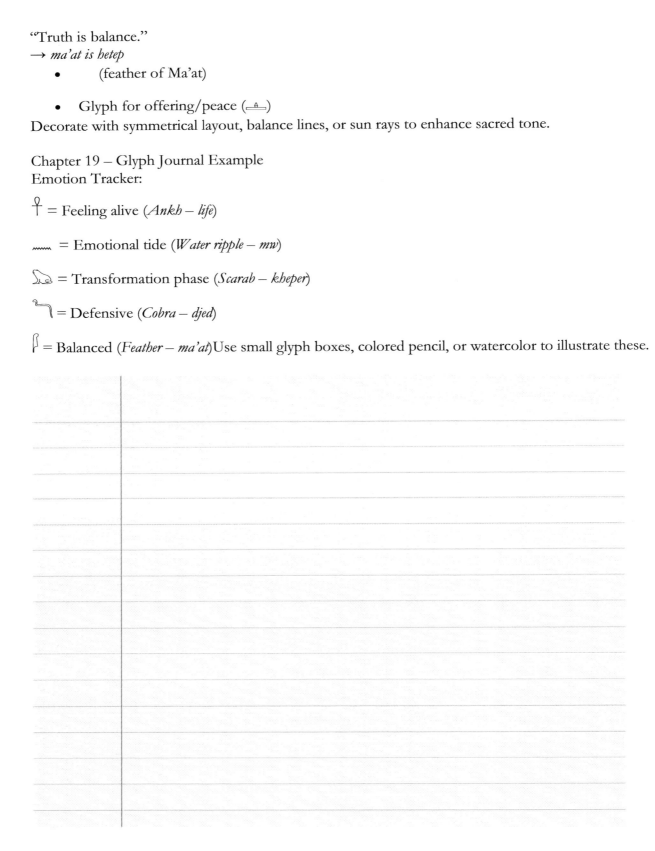

Appendix I: Common Verbs

Glyph	Transliteration	Meaning		Glyph	Transliteration	Meaning	
	r	to	do/make		ḏi	to	give
	nfr	to	be good		d	to	say
	t	to	take		ḥ	to	strike
	kꜣ	to	protect		m	to	come
	ỉ	to	go		ḥ	to	be
	mꜣꜥ	to	see		sḏm	to	hear
	mr	to	love		rḫ	to	know
	ḥqꜣ	to	rule		sḏꜣ	to	obey
	kꜣ	to	protect		nḥj	to	swim
	ḫwꜥ	to	jump		ḫn	to	find

FINAL EXAM: Decoding the Offering Formula

BM EA 558 – A Masterclass in Ancient Expression

You've come a long way. You've drawn glyphs, built sentences, read inscriptions. Now it's time to put it all together with one of the most famous and commonly repeated inscriptions in all of ancient Egypt. This will require all of the skill sets you have developed so far!

The Offering Formula

Found on tombs, stelae, and statues, this formula is a message from the living to the dead—and to the gods. Think of it as an ancient, magical care package.

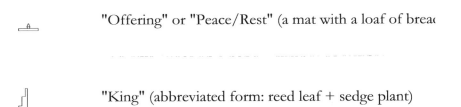

ꜥ htp-dỉ-nsw – "An Offering Which the King Gives"

Let's start with the first—and most iconic—phrase in the formula:

ḥtp-dỉ-nsw
Translation: *"An offering which the king gives"*

This phrase is actually four ideas packed into three glyphs:

"Offering" or "Peace/Rest" (a mat with a loaf of bread

"King" (abbreviated form: reed leaf + sedge plant)

The full phrase means "An offering which the king gives", but more than a translation, it's a ritual invocation. It begins the spiritual transaction, like saying "May the king authorize this offering to the god…"

To Whom? → Osiris, Lord of Djedu

Now the recipient of this royal gift:

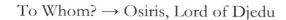

Wsir nb Djedu

- Wsir (◡ı): Osiris

- nb (◡): Lord

- Djedu (𓊽𓏲𓈖𓈖𓈉): The city of the Djed pillar = Busiris, Osiris' cult center

- Town or place determinative (⊗) not spoken, a symbol that the word is a place or town

This is Osiris in his formal capacity as **"Lord of Djedu"**, his power center.

Then it continues:

nṯr ꜥꜣ nb Abdw
= *Great god, lord of Abydos*

Abydos can be spelled with or without the (⊗) town determinative and in two different common spellings :

The Main Offerings (What's Being Given?)

After invoking Osiris, we get the real gift list:

Bread, Beer, Ox, Fowl, Alabaster, Linen, Everything Good and Pure

Let's break it down:

Item	Glyph	Transliteration	Notes
Bread		*T*	Standard loaf of bread glyph
Beer		*Hnqt*	Jug and determinatives for liquid

Item	Glyph	Transliteration	Notes
Ox		k	Often drawn as a bull with horns
Fowl		Pd	Duck-like bird, roasted offering
Alabaster		$\check{S}ss$	Stone vessel
Linen		hsb	Cloth roll with ties
Everything Good		$nb\ nfr\ w'b$	"Everything good and pure"

Pure can also be written with an ideogram:

Together, this list represents **the ideal offering bundle**—all the essentials needed to sustain a ka (soul): food, drink, ritual purity, and luxury.

The Gift's Purpose: A Voice for the Dead

So that he may give a voice offering...

This next phrase is often:

Or abbreviated to:

"r ḏỉ ḫꜣt ḥr"
= *"So that he may give a voice offering of..."*

"Voice offering" is symbolic. The ancient Egyptians believed that **just speaking the formula aloud was enough to conjure the offering.**

Alternative "King" Writing

Sometimes the word for king is written the reed ( ):

- **Reed leaf (⸖) =** *s*

- **Loaf (⌒) =** *t*

- **Water ripple (⌇) =** *n*

These form the word **nsw** (king) in a more abstract, phonetic style: ⸖⌒⌇

The Final Dedication: For the Ka of…

Ц⌐ = *ka* (life-force or soul)
The formula usually ends with:

Ц⌐ ⌐⌇ ⌒
= "for the ka of the revered one [name]"

Why This Formula Matters

This is not just a prayer. It's **an insurance policy for the afterlife**, carved in stone. It ensured the dead would be spiritually sustained forever. These formulas were believed to be self-activating: speak them, and the magic worked.

They appear all over Egyptian tombs and stelae—museum-goers walk by them every day, often unaware of their power, poetry, and purpose.

Let's break it apart in full:

Word-by-Word Breakdown

Let's break it apart, step-by-step, just like translating a sentence from Latin or French—but using ancient Egyptian.

1. ⌒⌐⌐ — ḥtp dỉ nsw

"An offering which the king gives"

- ⌂ (ḥtp): offering, rest, peace — a mat with a loaf

- ⌒ (dỉ): to give — the giving loaf

- ⌡⌡ (nsw): the king — sedge plant, abbreviated form

This phrase acts as the ritual opening, authorizing the spiritual gift.

---

2. ⌐ — nṯr

"To the god"

- ⌐ (nṯr): god — a flag on a pole (symbol of divinity)

Usually implied as the recipient of the offering.

---

3. ⌐⌐ — Wsir nb Ḏdw

"Osiris, lord of Djedu"

- ⌐ (Wsir): Osiris

- ⌒ (nb): lord (because it comes first, if it came after it would mean "thing")

- ⌐ (Ḏdw): Djedu (Busiris), Osiris' city

This section identifies which god is receiving the offering: **Osiris in his role as lord of Djedu.**

---

4. ⌐ — nṯr ꜥȝ nb Abdw

"The great god, lord of Abydos"

- ⌐ (nṯr): god

- ꜥꜣ (ꜥꜣ): great
- ꜣbdw (Abdw): Abydos (written with without a city determinative)
- nb (nb): lord

NOTE: Abydos can be written with or without the determinative for town (⊗)

Further describes Osiris' authority over Abydos.

---

5. ⟶ r

"So that" or "that he may…"
Marks the purpose or result of the preceding invocation.

---

6. ⟶ di

"May he give"

- Often follows *r* and is part of the voice offering clause.

---

7. ⟶ t, ḥnqt, kꜣ, pd, šss, ḥsb

"Bread, beer, ox, fowl, alabaster, linen"

- (t): loaf — bread
- (ḥnqt): beer (or jug glyph)
- (kꜣ): ox

- 🐦 (*pd*): bird or duck — fowl

- ⎰ (*šss*): alabaster

- ⌐⌐⌐ (*ḥsb*): linen (cloth roll)

These are the **six essential offerings** in tomb inscriptions. They provide nourishment, comfort, and purity in the afterlife.

---

8. 🔶🐦🦅 — **nb nfr wʿb**

"Everything good and pure"

- 🔶 (*nb*): all/every (or use the basket without a handle glyph)

- ⌐ (*nfr*): good, beautiful

- 🦅 (*wʿb*): pure (or use the foot with water jaw on top glyph (🔶))

This is a **generalization clause**, covering anything else the spirit may need.

---

9. ⌐ — **r**

"for…"

---

10. ⊔ — **ka**

"the soul, life-force"
The recipient of the offering is now identified.

---

11. 🔶🦅 — **imȝḥw**

"The revered one"

- *im³ḫw*: one who is "true of voice," a person whose soul is justified in the afterlife.

Final Translated Recap

"An offering which the king gives to Osiris, lord of Djedu, the great god, lord of Abydos, that he may give a voice offering of bread, beer, ox, fowl, alabaster, linen, and everything good and pure on which a god lives, for the ka of the revered one."

This offering formula is a **complete spiritual gift**, carved to last eternity.

BONUS: How to Impress Friends and Make Connections with Hieroglyphs

(Because Being Able to Write Names Like an Ancient Scribe is Pretty Cool)

Picture this: you're at a coffee shop, in a study group, or maybe even standing in line at a museum. You pull out a pen and casually doodle a seated owl, a loaf of bread, a wavy line. Someone leans over and asks, "What's that supposed to be?"

You look up and say, "Oh, that's your name… in ancient Egyptian."

Boom.

You've just won the moment.

This chapter isn't about dusty textbooks or grammar charts. It's about using your knowledge of hieroglyphs in a fun, meaningful, and totally charming way. Because let's face it—knowing how to write someone's name in a 5,000-year-old script is a total conversation starter.

Why It Works

People love to see their names turned into something visual. It's universal. Calligraphy, graffiti, tattoos, monograms—names have power. And Egyptian hieroglyphs don't just write names—they elevate them. They wrap them in mystery, in history, in magic.
And once you understand the basics (which you now do), you can easily become the go-to person for "Can you do my name next?"

Whether you're at a classroom event, a comic convention, an art night, or just doodling on a napkin, this is a simple way to:
- Connect with new people
- Make old friends feel special
- Show off your knowledge in a subtle (and fun) way
- Start amazing conversations about Egypt, language, and symbolism

It's the modern version of being a court scribe. And the best part? You don't even need ink and papyrus—just a pen and a little confidence.

Making the Magic Happen

Here's how it usually unfolds, organically and effortlessly.

You're sitting at a table with friends or new acquaintances. Someone pulls out a notebook. You ask, "Want to see how your name would look in hieroglyphs?"
They laugh—"You can do that?"

You nod and explain: "Well, not every letter exists in Egyptian, but I can transliterate the sounds." You write their name in uniliterals, maybe sketch a cartouche around it, and maybe even add a feather of Ma'at or the ankh for flair.

Within seconds, someone else is sliding their notebook your way.

Now you're the scribe of the table.

Transliteration On the Fly

Of course, you'll want to keep it simple at first. Use the uniliteral signs from Appendix A to spell out the phonetic equivalents of your friend's name. Remember: Egyptian didn't have letters like C, J, V, or X—so you'll need to substitute based on sound.

For example:

- "Jessica" becomes "J-E-S-I-K-A" → transliterated as: 𓄿𓇋𓇋𓊨𓎡𓏭

- "Mark" becomes "M-A-R-K" → 𓅓𓄿𓂋𓎡

- "Lily" becomes "L-I-L-I" → 𓂋𓇋𓂋𓇋 (since L = R in Egyptian)

- "Alex" becomes "A-L-E-K-S" → 𓄿𓂋𓇋𓎡𓋴

Add a cartouche for dramatic flair, and voilà—it's ancient personalized calligraphy.

Bringing the Conversation Deeper

Once someone's name is written, the fun continues. You can ask:
- "Want me to add a glyph that represents your personality?"
- "Do you want a symbol of protection, like a scarab or ankh?"
- "What's your favorite animal? I'll add it in the margin, Egyptian-style."

Suddenly you're no longer just writing letters—you're creating a personalized hieroglyphic talisman.

And more often than not, the next thing someone says is:

"Can I learn how to do this?"

And just like that, you've passed the scroll.

Real-World Examples

One high school teacher we spoke with used glyph-name writing as a weekly reward in class. Another artist at a comic convention offered to draw hieroglyphic nameplates for fans—many of whom ended up buying their art on the spot.

A museum guide started offering quick glyph demos during family programs, and it doubled their group engagement.

In every case, the result is the same: people are enchanted by seeing their own identity reframed through the lens of ancient Egypt.

You've taken something modern and made it feel eternal.

A Note on Cultural Respect

It's important to recognize that while this is fun and creative, we're dealing with a real and sacred writing system. When writing someone's name in hieroglyphs, treat it like calligraphy or a meaningful symbol, not a joke. Avoid using hieroglyphs in ways that mock or trivialize Egyptian beliefs or sacred figures.

Final Thoughts:

We started this journey with curiosity. With squiggles that looked like birds and eyes and suns. We learned to draw them, sound them out, read them, and now? Now we're sharing them.
And that's the best part.

Hieroglyphs are more than just an ancient writing system. They're a bridge. A doorway. A conversation starter between the past and the present, between you and someone who never imagined they'd see their name wrapped in a royal cartouche.
You don't need a degree to bring language back to life.
You just need a pen, a little practice… and a sense of purpose.

Whether you're looking to continue your studies, find your next artistic project, or connect with other glyph geeks, these resources are your gateway. Ancient Egypt is everywhere—in fashion, music, comics, museums, and your own imagination.

Please use the blank pages with lined notes to practice. I also highly recommend making flash cards of glyphs and vocabulary words.

Whatever you do, keep exploring. Keep creating.

And always… keep doodling with purpose!

About the Author

Scott Neitlich is a brand strategist, storyteller, and lifelong lover of ancient symbols. With over 25 years of experience across Fortune 500s, startups, and everything in between, Scott has launched iconic toy lines, revitalized digital platforms, and helped brands across entertainment, automotive, food service, and pharma grow with purpose.

Nicknamed the "Toy Guru," Scott has been a go-to voice in media and fan communities, recognized for his insights on toy trends, collector culture, and brand storytelling. He holds an MBA from the University of North Carolina, where he learned to bridge creative vision with business results.

But long before that, Scott stood in awe before the hieroglyph-covered temples of Egypt—a trip that ignited his lifelong fascination with ancient languages and visual storytelling. That spark eventually became *Doodling with Purpose*, a book born from academic curiosity, artistic wonder, and a little nerdy joy.

In 2024, he released *Myth Wars*, an AI-illustrated graphic novel reimagining the teenage years of the Greek gods (available now on Amazon).

Scott lives in Greensboro, North Carolina with his wife, daughter, and roughly 10,000 action figures.

TM and © Spector Creative. Photo taken by Author

AND: Check out the **SPECTOR CREATIVE** YouTube channel for the full *DOODLING WITH PURPOSE* video series! Featuring 200 companion videos to this book—each under 10 minutes!

Made in the USA
Middletown, DE
24 April 2025

74710798R10139